Bullied into Jail

A. Morris-Dadson

Names of people and places have been changed to protect the privacy of individuals.

ISBN: 0991761626
ISBN-13: 9780991761623

For Jim

"At Southern Ontario Hospital, we respect your right to the privacy of your personal health information.

As our patient, you, or a person legally acting on your behalf, entrust us with information about yourself. To honour that trust, we use and disclose your information for identified or primary purposes related to your care, and we protect it from misuse."

- *Southern Ontario Hospital*

"Deeds Speak"

- *Motto of Police*

"If the law supposes that," said Mr. Bumble, "the law is an ass – an idiot."

- *Charles Dickens,*
Oliver Twist

"Liberty lost is never regained and can never be fully compensated for."

- *Supreme Court of Canada (R v Hall)*

Contents

1.   Muriel 1

2.   Brad. 5

3.   Jane 7

4.   Bullies 13

5.   Unconfirmed 21

6.   A Cry for Help 25

7.   Southern Ontario Hospital 31

8.   Trevor 37

9.   Grad with Beautiful Beth 47

10. Summer. 53

11. Vacation 69

12. I Would Just Walk Away 75

13. That Guy 79

14. Shock. 83

15. Doing Hard Time 95

16. September 6 101

17. Cool Friends 105

18.   Changes. 109

19.   Fourteen 115

20.   September 13. 119

21.   September 18. 125

22.   House Arrest. 133

23.   PTSD and Panic Attacks. 141

24.   Holly and Daniel 145

25.   A Fresh Start. 151

26.   CAS and CAMH. 153

27.   Proceed by Indictment 159

28.   Prisoners 165

29.   The Trial 169

30.   Tell Me When It's Over. 197

31.   Epilogue 201

1.

Muriel

On a balmy June day, in the year 2004, a small girl and a tall boy were strolling along a sunny street eating Popsicles. Both were soon to leave childhood behind. The girl had an exquisite young face, framed by long, sun-streaked hair, and her expression was solemn, faintly wistful. She wore a light, cotton blouse and shorts on her slim frame and carried a pink backpack. The boy was handsome and self-assured. He wore faded jeans and a T-shirt bearing the name of a rock band, and his blond hair was tucked under a Toronto Maple Leafs cap. There was no traffic on the sleepy little road and the only sound was the slapping of the girl's flip-flops as she walked. Then, something else. The girl stopped to listen. "Do you hear that Mark?" she whispered. "Someone is crying."

"I think it's that old lady on the bench outside the nursing home," replied Mark. "Let's go over and see what's wrong."

They crossed the street and approached the hunched little figure apprehensively. She was wearing a grey tweed suit that smelled of lavender and mothballs. The girl joined her on the bench and smiled. "Hi, my name is Jane," she said, "and this is my cousin, Mark. Can we help you?"

The elderly woman dabbed her eyes with a tissue, then blew her nose. "I'm Muriel," she said, "Muriel Charlotte Smith."

"Would you like the other half of my Popsicle, Muriel?" offered Jane. "It's grape."

"Thank you. I would." Muriel gingerly took a small bite of the Popsicle. "I have nobody," she sniffed. "They're all dead, and I'll be next. And I have no grandchildren to visit me, like the others do. God help me, I have to live in this horrible place. I might as well be dead."

"We don't have any grandparents," Jane said softly. "We could be your grandchildren and come to visit you. Mark lives in Toronto but I live here in Allerton, so I could visit more often."

"How often will you come?" Muriel asked. She brightened. "Can I have your phone numbers in case I feel like having a chat? I'll tell the others that I have two grandchildren."

Jane took a candy wrapper and a pen from her backpack and carefully wrote her number on it. "Mine is long distance," said Mark. "So I'll call you if you give me yours." Muriel frowned and thought for a moment. "I'll find out what my number is and give it to you when you visit," she said with an apologetic smile.

Jane regarded the pale, mottled skin of Muriel's small hands with a mixture of sadness and resolve. "I always feel better when I wear nail polish," she said, flashing her bright blue finger nails. "Would you like me to do your nails when I visit?"

"Yes, that would be very nice. Do you have any pink nail polish? Pink has always been my favourite colour."

When Muriel seemed in better spirits the two cousins said goodbye.

"Don't forget me," she called after them.

The following day, Jane and Mark walked into the nursing home and introduced themselves to the receptionist as Muriel Smith's grandchildren. With a bemused smile, the woman leaned across the counter and asked their ages.

"I'm fourteen," answered Mark. "And Jane is twelve."

Muriel was called to the front desk and proudly escorted her grandchildren back to her small room. Upon entering, Jane admired an antique doll that sat on a pink chenille bedspread.

"She is a real Shirley Temple doll," said Muriel with pride. "My mother bought her for me when I was a little girl during the thirties."

"Cool," said Mark. "My mom loves Shirley Temple movies."

"I'll come and give you a manicure whenever you want," promised Jane, after painting Muriel's nails a brilliant shade of pink. "Just call me. And we bought you this matching lipstick too."

Muriel smiled. "Oh, I haven't worn lipstick in a long time," she chuckled, then slowly walked over to her dresser mirror and carefully applied it. "I wish I had a pink blouse to match," she muttered, lifting her chin and throwing her shoulders back.

"You look pretty," said Jane.

"Yes," agreed Mark. "You look good, Muriel."

"I'm going to hide my nail polish and lipstick right here," Muriel whispered as she carefully opened the drawer of a small nightstand beside her bed. "I wish it had a lock on it. An old man once stole a pair of my panties from the dresser drawer. And the woman in the room across the hall wandered in here stark naked one night, looking for her mother. I told her that her mother had certainly been dead for years and she should go back to her room and put on a nightgown. What a sight she was! I was terribly upset and couldn't eat my bedtime snack. This place is festooned with perverts and lunatics!"

"It must be scary living here," Jane said with a shudder.

Mark smiled and averted his eyes.

Muriel's newfound grandchildren visited as often as they could and talked with her frequently on the phone.

"I'm expecting a call from work," Jane's mother, Helen, said one evening. "Why don't you use the computer to chat with your friends, instead of the phone?"

"Jane, I hate living here," Muriel was saying. "They keep testing me to see if I've gone crackers. Today the doctor asked me if I knew the name of the Prime Minister. I told him it was Paul Martin and I'm not an imbecile!"

"I'm sorry Muriel. They shouldn't insult you like that. Anyway, it doesn't matter what they think. Mark and I know that you're smart. Can I call you later? My mom needs to use the phone."

Jane said goodbye and turned to her mother. "I was talking to Muriel, Mom. She's an old lady who lives in the Main Street Nursing Home. She has no grandchildren, so Mark and I have adopted her as our grandmother. Her eightieth birthday is next week and I need some money to buy her a gift. Can I please have an advance on my allowance?"

Helen hugged her daughter. "I'm so proud of you," she said.

On her next payday, Helen helped to choose a blouse for Muriel and Jane carefully wrapped it in pink birthday paper. She and Mark bought a card and wrote "Hooray you're 80!" on the inside.

Mark surprised his adopted grandmother with her favourite movie, *The Wizard of Oz* and a DVD player that his parents had used in their van during family driving holidays.

On her eightieth birthday, Muriel wore a new pink blouse with matching nail polish and lipstick while she and her grandchildren ate cake and watched *The Wizard of Oz* together. A card proudly displayed on her nightstand said "Happy Birthday Grandma."

2.

Brad

It happened in an old farmhouse on the Easter weekend of April, 2006.

As Brad lay on his grandparent's bed, Jane stood at the window watching the elderly couple below as they painstakingly planted flowers in their garden.

Jane had met Brad the previous month through their mutual friend, Rebecca. The two girls had been choosing ice cream flavours in a small shop in the town of Allerton, when the handsome seventeen-year-old had appeared and offered to pay for their purchases. Rebecca made the introductions as she wrapped a napkin around her chocolate ice cream cone. "Jane, this is my friend Brad. He lives in Woolton but comes to Allerton to visit his grandparents."

When Brad began phoning and emailing Jane, she was flattered and agreed to spend time with him when he was in town.

"I hope it's not too early to be planting flowers. Sometimes it snows in April," mused Jane. "Let's go outside and help your grandparents."

But Brad had other ideas. He motioned for her to join him on the bed, pulled her toward himself then thrust his hand down the front of her sweater. Jane was startled. "Hey, don't do that!" she said. He rolled over, pinning her underneath him, and began tugging at her track pants. "No, stop it!" she whispered, not wanting to disturb the elderly couple. "I don't want to do this. I'm only thirteen!"

Brad put his hand firmly over her mouth. "I'm doing it," he said.

Jane focused on the ancient floral wallpaper, large pink roses on a green background.

3.

Jane

In May of 2006, Jane was sitting at the kitchen table finishing her homework and contemplating the upcoming grade eight graduation, when she thought of Muriel. Hurriedly, she grabbed a new bottle of nail polish, then rushed out the door and over to Main Street. With a growing sense of dread, she realized it had been weeks since they had spoken.

Before anyone at the nursing home could stop her, she raced down the hallway and into Muriel's room, only to discover an elderly gentleman in a wheelchair who regarded her quizzically. The familiar pink bedspread was gone, replaced by a plaid comforter. Gone was the Shirley Temple doll. The staff explained, to the startled girl, that Muriel had moved away and they did not have a new address or phone number for her.

Jane and Mark called every nursing home listed in the phone book in search of their grandmother, but she was nowhere to be found.

The grade eight students of St. Joan of Arc Catholic School, in the town of Toxteth, had been the first to attend a new Junior High program after grade six. These had not been happy years for Jane. At first she had been excited about wearing the new uniform and going to school with teenagers but she soon found it to be a difficult adjustment. She missed playing in the St. Joseph schoolyard at recess time and it seemed, at age twelve, she was expected to grow up too quickly. After school, she still enjoyed riding her bike, rollerblading and playing with her dog in the park, but during school hours she felt a need to emulate the older girls in order to be accepted. It was comforting to know that her brother Chris attended the same school. She sometimes saw him in the hallways between classes, a tall, handsome boy with blond, disheveled hair, who always waved to her or smiled reassuringly.

Jane found pleasure in composing short stories and dreamed of writing movie scripts when she was older. Another leisure activity was going to the Toxteth movie theatre with friends. She loved fantasies and, next to the classic *Wizard of Oz*, her favourite movie was Tim Burton's animated story, *The Nightmare Before Christmas*. She had first seen it with Mark, who later gave her the DVD as a fourteenth birthday present in April, 2006. Fascinated by a cartoon character named Sally, a doll whose face was stitched from the corners of her mouth to her ears, Jane decided to paint her face as Sally for Halloween and Mark planned to be Jack Skellington, another *Nightmare Before Christmas* character with a stitched smile.

After Muriel disappeared from her life, Jane rarely used the telephone. She did not own a cell phone and, like many teenagers in 2006, communicated with her friends through MSN (Microsoft Network), an instant text messaging system on the internet. They found it liberating to have conversations among themselves using short forms for words that adults would not understand. The users invented special MSN names to identify themselves. Jane's alias was "sallythedoll" and her friend, Beth Henderson, called herself "highonlust." It was a secret world that seemed benign to the uninitiated. Helen was pleased that her daughter was able to talk with friends, near and far, without using the phone. She believed it to be harmless fun.

Beth Henderson was lucky. Or so it seemed to Jane. Beth and her older brothers lived in a large stately home near the school in Toxteth with their stay-at-home mom and a father who was successful and well respected.

Jane lived in a small bungalow in the town of Allerton with her mother, three older brothers, James, Joe and Chris, their little dog, Sandy and two cats named Jynx and Felix. On weekdays, she and Chris travelled eighteen kilometres by school bus to St. Joan of Arc in Toxteth, the closest Catholic school, while their mother drove forty kilometres to her job at the Newton courthouse.

Helen and her husband had separated when Jane was a baby and the family had not seen or heard from him in many years. She struggled to support herself and their four children on her meager salary and a small amount of self-employed income. By day she was a court reporter and during evenings and weekends she typed transcripts on a computer in her bedroom. Helen's small bedroom was crammed with her parents' teak bedroom suite, a desk, chair, computer, transcriber, printer, treadmill and small TV. She rarely had time to watch TV but used the treadmill faithfully every day in order to stay fit and keep her blood pressure down. It seemed to Jane that her mother lived in the bedroom, only emerging to drive to the courthouse.

Most of Jane's friends had fathers who doted on their daughters and used pet names for them, such as "princess" or "beautiful." One stocky, bespectacled girl named Amanda had a dad who regularly assured her that she was the prettiest, most talented girl in town. Amanda believed him. Jane had admired her self-confidence when, at a school Christmas concert, Amanda had performed a clumsy tap dance. As her thick legs pounded the stage and some members of the audience stifled the urge to laugh, Jane had watched Amanda's father smiling proudly and applauding his daughter.

After her parents' separation, Jane looked forward to occasional visits from her father. Then, inexplicably, after her seventh birthday, he vanished completely from her life. She and her brothers still received birthday cards from him most years but never Christmas cards or gifts. One Christmas, she had so desperately wanted her father to make a gingerbread house with her that she left dozens of telephone and email messages for him. He did not respond. And once she had sent him a long newsy letter and enclosed a school photo of herself, but never received an answer. She still hoped to see her father again someday.

In some respects it was a relief for Jane to put elementary school behind her. Never again would she be required to make a Father's Day card in art class. Well-meaning teachers had usually suggested that she make one for her mother.

After completion of the eighth grade, the students were to receive the sacrament of Confirmation at St. Joan of Arc Catholic Church. This was an important rite of passage from child to young adult in the Catholic faith. Each candidate was required to choose an adult sponsor for the occasion and Jane had given this honour to her Auntie Em. Father Luke, the parish priest, was to perform the ceremony on the fourth of June and Jane's mother had bought her a new white dress for the occasion.

However, in the minds of Jane and her friend, Beth, the main event was the graduation ceremony on June the twenty-third. There was to be a dance afterward and Jane happily announced on MSN that a classmate named Tim had asked her to be his date. But Beth seemed disinterested.

"Matt and I broke up," she said. "Would you go out with him if he asked you?"

"I don't know. Would you be mad if I did?" asked Jane.

"No, I wouldn't care, he's a dirty grease ball!" replied Beth.

Matt was a small, slim, athletic boy who usually wore a Boston Red Sox baseball cap. He interested Beth mainly because he attended Toxteth High School and, so, seemed worldly to a grade eight girl. He asked Jane if she would like to see a movie with him.

"Sure," she said, and offered to have her mother pick him up and drive them both to the movie theatre. "And my mom can give you a ride home afterward," she said. "Maybe she'll take us to the Dairy Queen for ice cream." She believed that Beth no longer had an interest in Matt.

Jane felt that Beth had everything necessary for a happy life and was mystified as to why she still seemed dissatisfied. Like a handful of other girls at school, Beth sometimes made superficial cuts to her arms and legs with a small knife. This was called being "emo," or emotional. Teen magazines had coined the term and reported that certain high profile musicians and movie stars were in the habit of cutting themselves. Thus, being "emo" had become trendy among a small number of suggestible teens. When Beth mentioned, on MSN, that she had cut herself, Jane expressed concern for her friend.

There was, at St. Joan of Arc Catholic School, a troubled girl named Nadia Reeves, one of Beth's many acquaintances. She was an older student who had earned the reputation of being a bully, a tough girl with no real friends. Beth befriended her and confided that a "slut" named Jane Collins, who regularly gave oral sex to boys, had stolen her boyfriend, Matt. She gave Nadia Jane's email address and MSN name and the bullying began.

4.

Bullies

It had been a long drive home from the Newton courthouse and Helen was exhausted. She just wanted to grab a bite to eat and scan the newspaper for a few minutes before retiring into her bedroom to type a large transcript for the remainder of the evening. She had received an urgent order from a judge who needed it the following morning. These requests sometimes meant working through the night. Upon opening the door, she was greeted by Sandy, a tan-coloured Cairn Terrier that had belonged to her late father. As her little dog leaped up and down barking excitedly, Helen noted that Jane was sitting in her usual spot at the family computer in the living room, Chris was listening to music and James and Joe were having a loud discussion in their basement bedroom. Sitting down with the newspaper, she noticed that her daughter looked pale and seemed to be trembling. She was teary-eyed as she typed a message on the computer.

"What's wrong sweetheart?" Helen asked.

"Nothing," replied Jane, switching off the computer. "We've already had dinner, Mom," she said, heading for her bedroom with Sandy. "I made spaghetti."

Helen felt guilty about being late again. She and her children seldom ate meals together anymore. James worked odd hours at a local restaurant and Joe, who was attending University, spent most of his time living in Toronto with her sister, Emily, and brother-in-law, Jack. She tapped on her daughter's door and poked her head into the room. Jane was sitting on the bed strumming her guitar and serenading Sandy.

"You're sounding very professional these days," Helen commented cheerfully.

Jane smiled. "I love playing the guitar Mom. Thanks for letting me take lessons. When I'm sad, I always feel better when I play my guitar. I think I sound pretty good. And I really like playing the piano too. I wish we had one at home so I could practice."

Although Jane's music lessons were a financial burden, Helen believed them to be as essential as the braces on James' teeth. Painfully aware that her children felt rejected by their father, she tried to do all she could to boost their self-esteem.

Satisfied that her daughter's mood had improved, Helen made a peanut butter sandwich and a cup of tea, then carried them into her bedroom and began typing. Chris was quietly working on a school project and the two older boys had gone out, James to his job at the restaurant and Joe to Toronto. Jane turned on the computer and logged onto MSN.

| Session start: Thursday, June 01, 2006
| Participants:
| sallythedoll
| highonlust

[07:08:20 PM] sallythedoll: did you give nadia my email?

[07:08:32 PM] highonlust: she asked for it, why?

[07:08:53 PM] sallythedoll: i don't know, she added me. i didn't accept it though, did she do it so she can make fun of me?

[07:09:07 PM] highonlust: i dunno haha, she just wanted it.

[07:09:14 PM] sallythedoll: Mmmmhmmm

[07:09:19 PM] sallythedoll: anyways whats up

[07:09:30 PM] highonlust: did you accept nadia? or no

[07:09:34 PM] sallythedoll: yeah but i'm going to delete her. she's just going to make fun of me

[07:10:23 PM] highonlust: nadia wants to talk. i've added her to the convo

[07:10:38 PM] sallythedoll: oh

[07:10:50 PM] candygirl: you can't run from me forever

[07:11:01 PM] sallythedoll: i don't ever KNOW who you are. how do you even know me?

[07:11:12 PM] candygirl: i know who you are and that's good enough. and i know of you and i hear about your stupid skeleton body being a piece of shit and you are a shitty friend and doing stupid ass shit

[07:11:33 PM] sallythedoll: to who?

[07:11:38 PM] candygirl: it doesn't matter to who

[07:11:44 PM] sallythedoll: yeah it does

[07:11:56 PM] candygirl: but whoever hangs out with that grease ball deserves to be hated

[07:12:21 PM] sallythedoll: thanks for standing up for me beth

[07:12:43 PM] highonlust: uhm, i'm not part of this Jane

[07:12:52 PM] sallythedoll: what is it ABOUT then

[07:13:08 PM] highonlust: like i said i'm not part of this and you should be standing up for yourself

[07:13:57 PM] sallythedoll: does this have to do with you

[07:14:26 PM] highonlust: what did i just say. you gotta learn to have self confidence Jane. having no self esteem makes you seem low

[07:14:41 PM] sallythedoll: what are you talking about

[07:14:51 PM] highonlust: you know what i'm talking about

[07:15:13 PM] sallythedoll: i didn't do anything to you

[07:15:20 PM] highonlust: wtf. i never said you did

[07:16:38 PM] sallythedoll: what did you tell her

[07:16:47 PM] highonlust: I didn't tell her anything. its called stories

[07:16:58 PM] sallythedoll: like what?

[07:17:16 PM] highonlust: i don't know. why are you asking me

[07:17:36 PM] sallythedoll: because you're her friend. you're the only one i know that talks to her

[07:17:59 PM] highonlust: that doesn't mean shit...srsly Jane

[07:18:20 PM] sallythedoll: what is this about

[07:19:10 PM] highonlust: wtf i have to go now. bye.

The following morning, Helen was exhausted. She had managed to finish the transcript but it had cost her a night's sleep. With an aching back and swollen feet, she wearily put the coffee on, tapped on Chris' door then went into Jane's room. She found her sleeping peacefully, one arm around Sandy. Quietly, she stood by the bed, admiring her daughter's delicate features. Looking at the faces of her children was a happy reminder of the importance of her life as a mother and breadwinner. Resisting the temptation to grab her camera, she realized that she had taken more than enough photographs of Jane and Sandy sleeping together over the years. Then she spotted sheets of paper on the nightstand, quickly read the short story and proudly wondered if her daughter might be a professional writer one day. Leaning over, she whispered, "Time to get up for school sweetheart. What would you like for breakfast?"

Sandy sprang to life and licked Jane's face. Reluctantly, she climbed out of bed, showered, pulled on her school uniform and tied her hair in a ponytail. After a quick breakfast she and Chris boarded the bus.

As she approached the school entrance, after saying goodbye to her brother, Jane heard snickering behind her back and the word "slut" being whispered. Then she felt wet splashes on her neck. She wondered if she had been spat upon but did not turn around.

Finally school was over for the week. Chris stayed in Toxteth to catch a movie and a bite to eat with a couple of friends and Jane warily took the school bus home without her brother. She was greeted at the door by Sandy who barked happily and fetched her leash. She took her little dog for a walk before the two settled down at the computer.

| Session start: Friday, June 02, 2006
| Participants:
| candygirl
| sallythedoll
| highonlust

[05:12:21 PM] candygirl: you have no class

[05:12:33 PM] sallythedoll: what do you want me to do

[05:12:40 PM] candygirl: watch yourself and what you do to people i'm friends with. your ignoring me won't help

[05:12:57 PM] sallythedoll: i didn't do anything to anyone

[05:13:22 PM] candygirl: you did

[05:13:28 PM] sallythedoll: what did i do

[05:13:32 PM] candygirl: you're a little tramp

[05:13:51 PM] sallythedoll: you don't even know me

[05:14:56 PM] candygirl: you make yourself look like a slut

[05:15:48 PM] sallythedoll: how is that hurting you? and i don't make myself look like a slut. i don't even know what this is about

[05:16:24 PM] candygirl: haha. its about you being a little loser try-hard

[05:16:33 PM] sallythedoll: what am i trying to be

[05:16:43 PM] candygirl: whatever everyone else is. srsly you will never win with me

[05:17:24 PM] sallythedoll: what do you want me to do

[05:17:30 PM] candygirl: die

[05:17:41 PM] sallythedoll: ok

[05:17:50 PM] candygirl: so hurry up and get on it because soon enough you'll be dying from aids anyways. i've never seen an aids victim but if I were to ever see one it would fit your description, and you know what else is shitty, is when you steal from people you call your friend.

[05:19:25 PM] sallythedoll: beth?

[05:19:34 PM] candygirl: i never said beth but knowing you, you probably did. you are a FAKE, theres nothing real about you

[05:20:22 PM] sallythedoll: and what does this make you?

[05:20:31 PM] candygirl: i'm real on the inside and out, just cause i wear makeup doesn't make me fake

[05:20:50 PM] sallythedoll: i don't know who you are

[05:20:58 PM] candygirl: i'm up front and honest and i don't steal. you're a lying try-hard wanna be thats never gonna be

[05:21:39 PM] sallythedoll: holy crap i never did anything to you or anyone

[05:21:50 PM] candygirl: YOU DID and you denying it won't fix the problem it just makes it shittier for you

[05:22:08 PM] sallythedoll: i don't even know what i did or who i did it to

[05:22:18 PM] candygirl: i told you whats wrong with you

[05:22:20 PM] sallythedoll: and who told you this

[05:22:25 PM] candygirl: it doesn't matter who told me

[05:22:32 PM] sallythedoll: kind of does

[05:22:35 PM] candygirl: its the fact you're like this and do stupid fucking shit

[05:22:48 PM] sallythedoll: what am i doing thats so stupid. you don't KNOW me

[05:23:05 PM] highonlust: but people know about you. just thought I'd throw that in.

[05:23:39 PM] sallythedoll: obviously they DONT

[05:23:56 PM] highonlust: i have to go now. my moms bi-otching.

5.

Unconfirmed

At six-o'clock in the evening, Sandy was sitting in her usual spot at the living room window waiting for Helen's car to pull into the driveway. Jane was in her bedroom wistfully studying a framed page from a colouring book that hung over her bed. It was signed "Jane and Grandma." She remembered happily colouring the picture with her grandmother when she was five-years-old. Grandma had been a devout Roman Catholic who never missed Sunday mass at St. Joan of Arc Catholic Church. Warmly, she recalled going to church with her grandmother, mother and brothers. In her mind's eye, she could still see the look of pride and joy on her grandmother's face as she watched James and Joe perform their duties as altar boys. Grandma had fully expected to witness the Confirmation ceremonies of all seven grandchildren, but had passed away just after the second eldest, Stephen, was confirmed. Jane wondered what her grandmother would think of her now.

Sandy began barking and ran to the door. Helen walked into the house with her arms full of plastic bags and handed them to Jane. "Put these groceries away please," she said, as she knelt down to greet her little dog.

"Father Luke said that I can't be confirmed this year," Jane said dejectedly. "I'm the only one in the whole class."

"What?" said Helen in surprise. "Why?"

"He said that because I skipped the preparation classes after school, I can't be confirmed with all of the other kids on Sunday, but I can do it next year if I go to the classes then. My white dress probably won't even fit next year. I already know all of the stuff they were teaching. I didn't need those stupid classes!"

"But if it was a requirement, then why didn't you go?" asked her mother.

"Because kids have been calling me names and spitting on me and laughing at me and threatening to beat me up, so I just wanted to come home after school," Jane cried as she ran to her room in tears.

The church secretary handed the phone to Father Luke.

"Hello," he said benignly. "May I help you?"

"Hello Father, my name is Emily Morrison and I am Jane Collins' aunt and Confirmation sponsor. I understand that there has been a misunderstanding regarding Jane's Confirmation this Sunday."

"No, there has been no misunderstanding, Mrs. Morrison. Jane did not attend the compulsory preparation classes, so I am afraid that she cannot be confirmed this year."

"Please consider making an exception in her case, Father. She was being bullied by other children and was afraid to attend the classes. She knows the material that was taught. Perhaps she could meet with you and be tested on it."

"No, that would not be fair to the other students."

"I know that exceptions are made, Father," persisted Emily. "My son, Stephen, has autism and did not attend Confirmation classes, yet he was confirmed along with his classmates."

"That was a different situation. Your son has a disability. Jane does not," sighed Father Luke.

"Yes she does," argued Emily. "She is suffering from anxiety and low self-esteem as a result of being bullied by those saintly kids who attended your Confirmation classes."

"Mrs. Morrison, special arrangements need to be made in advance," said Father Luke, who was losing his patience. "The Confirmation is this Sunday. I am sure that, in your son's case, the priest was made aware well in advance."

"Please Father," pleaded Emily. "I'm telling you now that this is a child who suffers from anxiety, depression and low self-esteem. She has been bullied by her classmates. If she is excluded from the Confirmation ceremony, it may have a devastating impact on her."

"I said no, Mrs. Morrison. I must abide by the rules of the church," said Father Luke sanctimoniously.

"Well, why don't you ask yourself, what would Jesus do?" suggested Emily. "Would Jesus turn his back on a disturbed child, Father?"

"Now you are insulting me Mrs. Morrison. Good Day to you."

"I hope you burn in hell!" shouted Emily as she slammed the phone down in despair.

Two days later, during a joyous ceremony at St. Joan of Arc Catholic Church, all, but one, of the grade eight students were confirmed by Father Luke. Jane stayed home and took a combination of two over-the-counter painkillers.

That afternoon, regardless of Father Luke and the church, Auntie Em, Uncle Jack, Mark and Stephen drove to Allerton with a Confirmation cake and a gift for Jane, but she was in bed, asleep and too ill to eat anything.

"She must have the flu," said Helen as she served the cake.

6.

A Cry for Help

It seemed to Jane that most of her friends had deserted her. She was aware of a rumour circulating around the school that she was a slut who gave oral sex to boys. No one would join her for lunch in the cafeteria and she felt all eyes were upon her as she carried her tray of food to a table. As she sat down, a group of nearby girls picked up their lunches and, with a dramatic flourish, moved away from her. She dreaded eating alone and it seemed that every mouthful of food she ate elicited giggles and whispers. As she chewed her sandwich self-consciously, she scanned the cafeteria for Nadia Reeves. Her only friend, Matt, had warned that this girl was planning to beat her up.

After lunch, as she walked down the school hallway, she heard laughter behind her back. Someone whispered, "Jane Collins gave Matt a BJ." She did not turn around but ran toward her locker to grab some books for the next class. As she stood nervously spinning the combination needle on her lock, Monica Johnson, a large, red-haired girl, gave her a forceful shove. As she struggled to regain her balance, Jane spun around and came face to face with Nadia Reeves. Then she was surrounded. Nadia, Monica, Amanda and a couple of other girls grinned at her.

"You're a piece of shit."

"You have no friends."

"You're a slut."

"Shut up!" shouted Jane. "Leave me alone!"

Just then, Miss Kelly, the English teacher appeared. "Jane Collins, you know better than to shout like that in the corridor," she scolded. The group of girls smirked and shook their heads. It seemed to Jane that everyone in the school had turned against her, even Miss Kelly.

"Fuck off!" she screamed at the teacher.

"Three days in the suspension room," said Miss Kelly.

As she sat in the suspension room trying to concentrate on her schoolwork, a group of girls made nasty gestures and faces at Jane through the window.

Chris was in grade twelve and often remained in Toxteth with friends after school to have dinner at McDonald's or go to the movie theatre. There was not much for teenagers to do in Allerton. Fearful that, without her brother for protection, she would be bullied on the school bus, Jane arranged for Matt to meet her after school and escort her to his house. There she could safely wait for her mother to pick her up after work. As they walked toward his house, a group of Toxteth girls followed closely behind, spat at Jane and called her names.

Matt's mother made some mini pizzas and chocolate milk and the two friends played with Matt's baby brother and watched TV until Helen came to collect her daughter. As soon as they arrived home Jane logged onto MSN and Helen rushed back out to buy dog food for Sandy.

| Session Start: Wednesday, June 07, 2006
| Participants:
| sallythedoll
| highonlust

[05:57:18 PM] sallythedoll: so nadias going to beat me up?

[05:57:43 PM] highonlust: shes not gonna. and matt said you two are dating. why did you lie when I asked you then

[05:58:12 PM] sallythedoll: i didn't

[05:58:24 PM] highonlust: you said you guys aren't dating

[05:58:53 PM] sallythedoll: we're just friends. matt says nadia said shes going to beat me up. so is it true O_O

[06:02:30 PM] highonlust: i said no but like wtf leave me out

[06:02:50 PM] sallythedoll: what did i do to you

[06:03:01 PM] highonlust: I NEVER SAID YOU DID ANYTHING JANE. QUOTE ME ON THAT. NO YOU CAN'T CAUSE I NEVER SAID THAT.

[06:03:45 PM] sallythedoll: you didn't stand up for me when nadia said i should die. you said you're my friend and you're saying i have low self esteem, meanwhile, you're the one cutting yourself

[06:05:29 PM] highonlust: you fucking twist everything jane

[06:06:32 PM] sallythedoll: you and nadia can leave me alone, i didn't do anything to you

[06:06:50 PM] highonlust: i wasn't bitching at you jane

[06:07:12 PM] sallythedoll: i just said you can leave me alone. you and nadia can leave me alone, i didn't do anything to you. why does nadia hate me anyway. she wouldn't hate me for no reason

[06:07:33 PM] highonlust: just like she said in the convo. you have no self esteem and you're always copying people

[06:07:50 PM] sallythedoll: why did i hear that she was going to beat me up

[06:08:01 PM] highonlust: i dunno.

[06:08:11 PM] sallythedoll: I want my mom to come home

[06:08:20 PM] highonlust: gtg bye

That night, Jane went into her bedroom with Joe's pen knife and cut her legs. Sandy licked the wounds, and the tears.

The following morning Chris and Jane sat at the kitchen table dressed in their school uniforms, white golf shirts with SJA embroidered on them and grey pants. Helen sipped her coffee and watched with pride as they ate their bowls of Cheerios. They are so beautiful, she thought, they look like a TV ad for breakfast cereal. She waved goodbye as they ran to catch the school bus, unaware that anything was amiss.

During day two in the suspension room, Jane noticed a spot of blood on her grey pants and went to the office to ask for a Band-Aid. When Mrs. Mason, the guidance counsellor, noticed the wounds and asked for an explanation, Jane admitted that she had cut herself because kids had been bullying her. She realized her mistake when Mrs. Mason called the offending girls into her office and ordered them to apologize. This was probably the worst thing she could have done. Jane was mortified.

Helen was sitting in a courtroom recording the evidence of a witness in a trial when she was paged to take an urgent phone call from Mrs. Mason, who told her what had happened.

"I believe this is a cry for help, Mrs. Collins," she said breathlessly. "You should get immediate counselling for your daughter. If you take her to the emergency department at Southern Ontario Hospital, you can avoid the long wait typically encountered in this area."

7.

Southern Ontario Hospital

Helen was a good mother. She collected Jane at Matt's house then drove directly to Southern Ontario Hospital in Newton to get professional help for her daughter. She called her sons to let them know that she and Jane were on their way to the hospital and would not be home for dinner. The boys had been concerned about their sister, after finding Joe's pen knife on her bed and blood on the sheets and on Sandy's fur. They were relieved to hear that she was safe.

"Don't worry about us Mom," said Joe. "I'll make some burgers for dinner and feed the pets. See you guys later."

After a long wait in the emergency department, Jane was seen by Irene, a crisis worker. She felt comfortable talking with Irene and confided that girls were bullying her at school and on MSN, and that she was depressed because her friends had turned against her. An older girl had told her to die and so she had cut her legs. She whispered that a rumour was circulating around school that she had given oral sex to boys, and kids were calling her a slut. This made her feel low.

Irene asked Jane what kinds of activities made her feel self-confident. Proudly she talked of her guitar and piano lessons at

Reynolds Music and of her short stories and poetry. However, Irene wanted to focus on the current crisis.

"Have you ever attempted suicide?" she asked.

Jane admitted taking a combination of Tylenol and Benadryl on the weekend.

"History of self-harm," noted Irene on a Crisis Team Assessment form.

"Do you often think of dying?"

"Yes, every day."

"Have you thought of attempting suicide again, and if so, how would you do it?"

"I would get a knife from the kitchen, and cut my throat on my bed."

Irene shook her head as she made notes on the form then asked Jane if she had ever experimented with drugs or alcohol. Remembering that she had once, when in the seventh grade, taken a nearly empty bottle of Baileys to school at Christmas time, she replied, "Yes I have."

Jane then volunteered that she did not like eating in front of people in the school cafeteria.

"Possible eating disorder," Irene noted on the form.

When questioned about a possible family history of drug or alcohol abuse, Jane speculated that her dad might be an alcoholic, but explained that she had not seen or heard from him since 1999, when she was seven years old.

When asked about legal issues, she related the scary story of herself and her friend Hilary being "in trouble" the prior year. Hilary had suggested taking some spray paint from the local hardware store and using it on the outside walls of the school. Jane had seen some impressive graffiti on a TV show and wanted to try doing some creative work with spray paint. She had painted a chunky, stylized word "Pink" on the brick wall of the school and Hilary, who was supposed to write "Floyd," had sprayed a clumsy, artless word "cunt" beside it. Hilary and Jane had been caught by the police and ordered to write "sorry" letters as punishment for what they had done.

"Legal Issues: been charged with theft, possession of stolen goods and mischief to property," noted Irene in her report.

Helen was dismayed when Jane later told her of this confession during their car ride home. "Oh Jane," she sighed. "You really didn't need to tell Irene about that." As a court reporter, she understood that minor incidents, when written down, took on a more serious tone and could easily be misconstrued.

"What would you like to do about the bullies at school?" Irene wondered.

"I would like to kill all bullies," replied Jane offhandedly.

"How would you do this?" asked Irene.

"I guess I would stab them."

"What would you use?" asked Irene.

"A kitchen knife," replied Jane. She was tired and bored with this conversation and wanted to go home and see Sandy. She was also hungry and hoped that her mother would stop at McDonald's or Tim Hortons on the way home.

"Homicidal thoughts – has wanted to kill bullies. Homicidal Plan – wanted to stab them. Specificity of Homicidal Plan – get knife and stab them at school. Availability of Means – kitchen knife," wrote Irene in her report.

Before Jane left Southern Ontario Hospital, Irene insisted that she sign a "Child and Adolescent Crisis Safety Plan." *"I am going to sleep in the same room as my mom (bedroom) for the night. And if I feel like hurting myself I will talk to someone. (one of my three brothers or my mom)."* Irene added, *"In case of emergency, I will call 310 COPE or come back to the Emerg. Dept."* Finally, an appointment was made for her to be seen by a counsellor named Tracey Hogan at Southern Ontario Hospital the following day.

When Jane and Helen left Irene's office and walked out into the Emergency department waiting room, they were surprised to see James, Joe and Chris who had driven from Allerton in Joe's jeep to be with their sister. They each gave Jane a hug and the family left the hospital.

On Friday morning Helen sat in the hospital waiting room nervously thumbing through an ancient Chatelaine magazine as Jane met with Tracey Hogan. During the half hour car trip from Allerton to Newton, she had explained to Jane that it was important for her to feel comfortable talking with Tracey. "Her job is to help you," said Helen. "Just say whatever is on your mind. You can feel free to talk about everything that has been troubling you: the mean girls at school, kids spitting on you, the lies, and that older girl who keeps threatening you on MSN. Don't be embarrassed. She is a professional counsellor and everything you say will be kept secret between the two of you."

Tracey was not at all what Jane had expected. She had imagined that a counsellor would be a young woman with wild curly hair wearing big loop earrings and a long dress with hippie beads and sandals. She would sit with one leg curled under her and lean forward with a pleasant round face and a friendly smile. The woman who sat behind the desk wore a tailored suit and was not smiling. She grimly began to recite a seemingly prepared speech in a monotone as soon as Jane sat down. The robotic sound of her voice was so mesmerizing that Jane did not listen to the words being spoken. She focused on Tracey's wrinkled brow and was reminded of a disagreeable third grade teacher she once had.

Tracey became silent. It appeared that she was reading the report that had been written by Irene. Then, she looked up at Jane and asked about her "plan to kill bullies."

Following Tracey's example, Jane answered in a monotone. She said that she did not have a "plan" and was not going to do anything. When Tracey persisted, she said that she might do something if the kids at school did not leave her alone. "They don't know what they have done," she said. Tracey asked about her suicide attempt.

Jane said that she felt suicidal every day and had tried to kill herself at least five times, the last attempt being when she had cut her legs. Tracey then glanced down at Irene's notes and asked if she planned to use a kitchen knife to slit her own throat. "Yes," she replied.

Jane wanted to tell Tracey that she had been raped two months earlier by a boy whom she had trusted and had thought was her friend. She had been afraid to tell her mother because she felt somehow responsible for what had happened. She wanted to unburden herself but was unsure of how to broach the subject or explain how devastated and betrayed she felt.

"Even if the bullying stopped, I would still want to die," she said. "Boys upset me all the time and I worry about hurting their feelings...."

Tracey did not allow her to finish what she had been trying to explain. She interrupted with a question about drug use. In an effort to impress Tracey with her worldliness and knowledge, like the older girls at school, Jane invented a story about drugs.

"About a month ago, I took some drug that was laced with something and I was high for hours and then blacked out," she said, trying to sound bored.

Tracey had heard enough. She called Helen into the room and informed her that she would be paging Dr. Keita, the on-call psychiatrist, to have Jane admitted for a mental health assessment. Helen was dumbfounded. "But she has an appointment to speak with our family doctor tomorrow. Dr. March is aware that Jane is having problems at school and has prescribed a mild antidepressant to help her. I have confidence in Dr. March. She has known my daughter all of her life and if Jane needed psychiatric help, surely she would have given us a referral."

Helen felt that she was losing control and was beginning to wonder if she had made a mistake in bringing her daughter to the hospital for help. Although she and Dr. March had known Jane all of her life, Tracey, who had spent less than an hour with her, felt that she understood her best.

As a counsellor, Tracey did not have the authority to admit Jane to the hospital. She completed an application for a psychiatric assessment and then scribbled a few notes for the psychiatrist indicating that Jane had a homicidal plan to kill people and was also suicidal. Upon reading the notes and interviewing Jane, Dr. Keita became concerned that she might be a suicide risk. She met briefly with Helen, who had difficulty comprehending what was being said due to the doctor's thick accent. She did not fully understand that Jane was to be removed from her care and transported to a hospital in Toronto for a psychiatric assessment.

A large uniformed man from hospital security escorted mother and daughter to the emergency department. At this point, Helen realized that she had been stripped of her parental rights and that Jane's fate was beyond her control. "Oh my God," she whispered. "What have I done?"

Shortly thereafter, two attendants appeared and ordered Jane to lie down on a stretcher to be lifted into an ambulance. "But I'm not sick," she protested. When told that this was a requirement, she began to cry. "Can my mom come with me?" she pleaded.

"No," they answered. "She can follow us in her vehicle."

8.

Trevor

Helen's hands were shaking so badly that she had difficulty dialing Emily's number on her cell phone as she sat in her car. When Emily answered, she immediately recognized the panic in her sister's voice. She had heard it years before, when Helen had called from the same hospital to say, "Mum has taken a turn for the worse."

"Oh no," she said. "What has happened?"

"Jane has been taken away from me," sobbed Helen. "The counsellor at Southern Ontario Hospital thinks she's crazy and is having her admitted to Toronto Hospital. I guess there are no beds available at Southern Ontario. I had no idea that Jane was so disturbed, but then, I'm just her mother and Tracey Hogan is a professional."

"I don't believe there is anything wrong with Jane," Emily shouted angrily into the phone. "She just needs to get away from those creepy kids at school. How could they just take her away without your permission?"

"I don't know," cried Helen miserably. "I couldn't understand what the doctor was saying. She had a thick accent, African or something. Anyway, as we speak, Jane is in an ambulance being rushed to a psych ward in Toronto and I'm to follow behind in my car. Maybe I shouldn't have taken her for counselling. I thought I was being a responsible parent and doing the right thing. She must be so scared. She doesn't even have her pyjamas or a change of clothes."

"Let's meet and buy Jane some new pyjamas and clothes and take them to her tonight," suggested Emily. "We could bring her some books and magazines too. Toronto Hospital isn't far from me. I take Stephen there for his hearing tests."

"What if they won't let you come inside with me?" Helen worried as she and Emily drove along the highway. "They might have strict rules about immediate family only."

"I'll wait outside for you," said Emily. "I don't mind."

"But I want you to come in with me. I hate being a single parent. I'm always going to teacher's meetings and doctor's appointments on my own. You're so lucky to have Jack."

"Well then, I'll tell them that we're a lesbian couple and I'm Jane's other mom," said Emily.

A guard opened the door to the psychiatric unit. As he escorted Helen and Emily along the quiet hallway, they noticed a young boy, perhaps a little older than Jane, pacing up and down. "At least there are other children here on weekends," Helen commented. The guard showed them to Jane's room and waited outside.

"That man is always watching me," Jane told them. "I don't mind though. I like it here. I feel really safe being so far from home."

As Helen and Emily were being escorted to the door, after their visit, Jane called out, "Don't worry Mom, everything will be okay. Thanks for the cool sweater Auntie Em. I love American Eagle stuff."

On Saturday, Jane met Trevor. He had been in the unit for a few days and told her that during the week he attended classes with other kids at the hospital so that he would not miss any schoolwork but on weekends most of the others went home and it was pretty boring. Jane thought he was cute in an unusual sort of way. He had shoulder length brown hair and a sprinkling of freckles over his round face. He was a tall, heavy-set boy who looked older than his thirteen years and towered over Jane who weighed only ninety pounds. Trevor told her that he needed to inject himself with Insulin because he was diabetic and that he also took a drug called Ritalin to calm him down. He boasted that he sometimes mixed Ritalin with a drug called Ecstasy and it gave him awesome hallucinations. Jane was not sure that she believed this story. When he said that he was a drug dealer being hunted by drug lords, she definitely did not believe him but was impressed with his wild imagination. He was a kindred spirit.

"And I sometimes break into cars and steal stuff," he volunteered.

Jane did not believe this either but thought it sounded intriguing. She hoped that he would invite her to spend some time with him at his home in Toronto. It would be a different world, far from the bullies of Toxteth.

Saturday was an agonizing day for Helen as she paced around the house worrying about her daughter's sanity. Her little dog followed her back and forth. Surely Tracey Hogan would not have done something so drastic unless it had been absolutely necessary, she thought as she opened the door to let Sandy out into the backyard. Then, walking past the kitchen window, something caught her eye. It was black and white. Joe, who had been outside washing his jeep, let out a blood curdling scream. "Holy crap!" he yelled. "Sandy's been sprayed by a skunk!"

Joe carried poor Sandy into the bathroom and placed her into the tub. Helen grabbed some shampoo and the two of them scrubbed the little dog's tan fur. It was futile. Sandy smelled terrible and so did they. Helen quickly showered and washed her hair before heading to the hospital to visit Jane.

"How are you sweetheart? We all miss you," said Helen as she hugged her daughter.

"Eeww Mom, you smell skunky," Jane said with a laugh. "Did you get sprayed by a skunk?"

"No, but Sandy did."

Jane was anxious to tell her mother about her new friend. "Guess what Mom," she said. "I met a really nice boy named Trevor. Kids at his school bully him too. He lives in Toronto. If he invites me to his house can I go? Please, please!"

"We'll see."

As she drove home that afternoon, Helen was stopped by the police and given a speeding ticket. I guess I'm just having one of those lives, she thought dejectedly. Later that night she received a long distance phone call from Jane.

"What's wrong sweetheart, is everything okay?" she asked worriedly.

"Sure Mom, everything is fine. I just wanted to tell you that after you left the hospital, they sprayed the entire third floor with something to get rid of the skunky smell. Isn't that funny?"

Early Monday morning Helen drove to the hospital in Toronto and met with Dr. Lee Cohen, a psychiatrist who had interviewed Jane. "I really don't know why your daughter was admitted to our psychiatric unit last Friday," the doctor said. "She has no psychiatric problems and is simply reacting to bullying at school."

Jane was released from the hospital. "Can I take the day off school Mom?" she asked. "I don't want to walk in late. Everyone would stare at me."

Helen felt a wonderful sense of relief as she drove her daughter home from Toronto. She felt so light hearted that she stopped at the mall and bought Jane a McDonald's "Happy Meal" and some new clothes that she could ill-afford. When they arrived home there was a phone message from Tracey Hogan advising that she would be going to Jane's school on Friday, June 16th and had made a referral for her to be assessed at Southern Ontario Hospital by a psychiatrist named Dr. Larry Feldman. Helen's heart sank.

Jane spent a relaxing Monday playing her guitar, rollerblading and taking Sandy for a walk. Late in the afternoon, she logged onto MSN to tell Beth about her new friend.

```
---------------------------------------------
| Session Start:  Monday, June 12, 2006
| Participants:
| sallythedoll
| highonlust
---------------------------------------------
```

[05:06:39 PM] sallythedoll: hey whats up

[05:07:05 PM] highonlust: why weren't you at school

[05:07:12 PM] sallythedoll: hospital

[05:07:20 PM] highonlust: O WHY

[05:07:37 PM] sallythedoll: i'll tell you tomorrow

[05:09:12 PM] highonlust: so are you going to school tomorrow?

[05:09:47 PM] sallythedoll: yes why

[05:10:12 PM] highonlust: just wondering

[05:10:25 PM] highonlust: write me a note about the hospital thing and i'll write you back

[05:10:37 PM] sallythedoll: what if people see

[05:11:09 PM] highonlust: i promise i won't show anyone. i always write notes with people.

[05:11:56 PM] sallythedoll: so whats new

[05:12:20 PM] highonlust: haha uh nothing much. you?

[05:12:29 PM] sallythedoll: i met a really nice guy named trevor. he's awesome

[05:13:14 PM] highonlust: at the hospital?

[05:13:20 PM] sallythedoll: yes ^_^

[05:13:33 PM] highonlust: why was he there, is he hot? lmao

[05:13:44 PM] sallythedoll: he is in his own way

[05:13:54 PM] highonlust: are you still dating matt?

[05:14:08 PM] sallythedoll: yes we're still friends

[05:14:44 PM] highonlust: what about trevor

[05:15:01 PM] sallythedoll: he lives in Toronto

[05:16:42 PM] highonlust: if he's really nice, maybe you should forget about matt..cause i know you like matt and all but when I was with him, he made me so miserable.. and i don't want that to happen with you. and i think matt is sex crazed..he wants sex. and he lies. and i'm not just saying this cause i don't like him. don't tell him i'm telling you this.

[05:18:10 PM] sallythedoll: o_O I won't. have you seen the movie Edward Scissorhands?

[05:18:22 PM] highonlust: no gtg bye

| Session Start: Wednesday, June 14, 2006
| Participants:
| sallythedoll
| highonlust

[05:44:24 PM] sallythedoll: hey

[05:45:49 PM] highonlust: whats up

[05:46:10 PM] sallythedoll: i'm on the phone with trevor. me and matt broke up

[05:46:32 PM] highonlust: you still have to write me a note about the hospital

[05:46:42 PM] sallythedoll: when are exams

[05:47:02 PM] highonlust: next week i think. are you getting your hair and makeup done for graduation

[05:47:26 PM] sallythedoll: if my mom will let me

On Friday evening, Helen asked Jane about her meeting with Tracey at school.

"It was okay I guess," she replied. "Tracey said that she goes to my school all the time and talks to other kids who have issues. She lives in Toxteth, so she doesn't mind seeing kids at SJA instead of the hospital. Maybe she likes going to my school because it's close to home and she gets to leave early."

"What did the two of you talk about?"

"Oh, nothing much, I just told her that Beth and I made up."

"You mean that you and Beth are friends again?"

"Yeah, we're good. Can Trevor come to Allerton for the weekend? It's so boring around here."

Helen phoned Trevor's mother and the two women agreed to meet at the Mall in Newton on Saturday. Mrs. Brown, a pleasant sounding woman with an English accent, seemed delighted that her son had been invited to spend the weekend with Jane in Allerton. Helen was impressed that she had offered to meet halfway. Usually Helen was the parent who picked up Jane's friends and drove them home.

When they met at the mall on Saturday, Helen recognized Trevor as the boy she had seen pacing the halls of Toronto Hospital when she had visited Jane. Although he was a big, heavy boy, he had a round baby face and it was obvious from his demeanor that he was only thirteen. Helen hoped that he would be a nice friend for Jane. Mrs. Brown explained that, because her son was diabetic and hyperactive, he required Insulin injections and a drug called Ritalin. "Behave yourself, Trevor," she said, as she climbed back into her car, "and don't forget to take your medication."

As Mrs. Brown drove away, neither she nor Helen suspected that, in addition to the Insulin and Ritalin, Trevor's backpack contained another drug that he intended to share with Jane. Helen was unaware of the mistake she was making in allow-

ing her daughter to associate with a boy whom she had met in
a hospital psychiatric unit. It was unfortunate that Tracey had
arranged for Jane to be admitted to such a place and it was unfortunate that, as a result, she had met Trevor.

```
--------------------------------------------------
| Session Start:  Sunday, June 18, 2006
| Participants:
| sallythedoll
| highonlust
--------------------------------------------------
```

[04:46:11 PM] highonlust: janeeee how are you

[04:46:23 PM] sallythedoll: sad because trevor's mom just picked him up.

[04:46:34 PM] highonlust: i'm downloading an avril lavigne song (yay) lmao

[04:46:44 PM] sallythedoll: oh lalala

It was Thursday, the twenty-second of June when Helen
opened the door of Dr. Feldman's office and was confronted by
a stern looking man who motioned for her to halt. He pointed
to the mat in front of his door. Helen and Jane wiped imaginary
dirt from their shoes and entered the room.

Jane had been surprised by Tracey's appearance but Dr. Feldman looked just as she had imagined. If I were making a movie,
she thought, I would definitely cast him as the psychiatrist. She
guessed him to be about the same age as her Uncle Jack, and he
had a beard too but, unlike Uncle Jack, Dr. Feldman did not have
a round friendly face. As he regarded Jane with his piercing eyes,
she had the uncomfortable feeling that he could read her mind.
As she scanned the sparsely furnished office, trying to avoid his

gaze, she was startled when her eyes came to rest upon bare feet inside a pair of sandals under his desk.

Dr. Feldman explained that during their next few sessions he would be doing a mental health assessment of Jane. This would involve separate interviews with Helen and Jane as well as joint sessions. After a brief discussion, Helen and Jane left his office and drove to Toxteth for Jane's regular Thursday afternoon music lesson at Reynolds.

9.

Grad with Beautiful Beth

J ane was in a cheerful mood during the drive home to Allerton. Mr. Reynolds had complimented her piano playing of "That Easy Waltz" without any mistakes, and she had, for the first time, used both hands at once. She was beginning to feel less anxious about graduation the following day and was proud that Tim had asked her to be his date for the dance afterward. As soon as her mother parked the car in the driveway, she ran into the house and excitedly logged onto MSN to talk with Beth about graduation plans. Sandy barked happily and sat down beside her chair. As she patted her dog's head, Jane stared at the computer screen in disbelief. Beth had changed her MSN name to "gradwithtim" and Tim's new moniker was "gradwithbeautifulbeth."

| Session Start: Thursday June 22, 2006
| Participants:
| sallythedoll
| gradwithtim

[05:43:50 PM] sallythedoll: oh you're going to grad with tim?

[05:44:10 PM] gradwithtim: yeah are you mad at me

[05:45:27 PM] sallythedoll: no. me and tim were going to go together but i don't care

[05:46:08 PM] gradwithtim: so you wouldn't be mad if i went with him?

[05:46:18 PM] sallythedoll: nope i don't care

[05:46:48 PM] sallythedoll: so did he ask you?

[05:47:01 PM] gradwithtim: sorta both of us. i dunno lol.

[05:47:55 PM] sallythedoll: Ohhh, how does that work

[05:48:19 PM] gradwithtim: I dunno. haha.

[05:48:52 PM] gradwithtim: are you mad at me tim-ee? ps; i like your msn name

[05:49:01 PM] gradwithbeautifulbeth: no

[05:49:22 PM] sallythedoll: like I mean he only wanted to go with me because he felt sorry for me. WHO does that? and you both like each other when i was supposed to go with him. i'm not begging on my knees but thats pretty rude i'm not mad at you i'm mad at tim.

[05:50:13 PM] gradwithtim: haha oh well tim said you guys weren't going out and he sorta asked me and i'm like well not if Jane's mad and shit. and you said you aren't so yeah sorry. are you gonna dance with tim?

[05:50:38 PM] sallythedoll: no i don't like him anymore, at all

[05:51:06 PM] gradwithtim: my grad dress is black with silver sparkles. i'm getting my hair cut and perfectly straightened and my makeup done.

[05:51:21 PM] sallythedoll: thats going to look really good.

Seeing Jane in tears again at the computer, Helen quietly read the new MSN names over her daughter's shoulder and was disheartened by the cruelty of Beth and Tim.

"Mom, I don't want to go to grad," Jane said. "Everyone will just laugh at me."

"No they won't sweetheart. We'll go shopping for a new dress and you can have your makeup and hair done professionally. You'll look awesome and Tim will be sorry that he didn't go with you."

When Jane later logged onto MSN, another classmate, Trevor Allen, who had viewed the previous exchanges with Beth and Tim, began a conversation with her.

"Since you won't be going to grad with Tim, would you like to go with me?" he asked.

"You don't need to ask me just because you feel sorry for me," Jane replied.

"I'm not. I'd like to go with you."

"Okay. I'll see you there."

The following day everyone gathered at the local arena for the Grade Eight Graduation. Jane was nervous and worried that her schoolmates might laugh at her when she walked on stage to receive her diploma, but was glad that she had so many family members for support. Her mom was there of course, and her brothers Chris, James and Joe with his girlfriend Kate. Auntie Em, Uncle Jack, Mark, Stephen, Uncle Jack's sisters Grace and

Josie, with her daughter Jackie, had all come to help celebrate the occasion. Jane was pleased that a couple of her classmates had commented on Mark. "Wow, he's hot! Is he with you Jane?"

"I wish my dad could be here," Jane whispered to Mark, "and Muriel too. I called the nursing home again but they still wouldn't tell me where she went. All of the other kids have their fathers and grandparents with them."

"Not everyone Jane," replied Mark. He feared the nursing home staff was simply being kind in saying that Muriel had moved away. He kept this thought to himself.

Jane's new dress was aqua with silver flecks. She loved it until, to her horror, she saw that Beth was wearing the same dress in black.

"Beth will think I copied her on purpose," she whispered to no one in particular. "The black dress looks way more elegant than mine."

"Which girl is Beth?" Auntie Em asked.

When Jane pointed her out, Emily shook her head in disbelief. Beth was a very average looking girl with wispy, poker straight black hair and black framed glasses. The black dress was too tight and emphasized her wide hips and thighs. She was holding court among friends and admirers and had an unmistakable air of superiority.

Jane stood with Mark. The aqua dress hung beautifully on her slim frame and her French-braided hair looked lovely. She had a flawless complexion and Emily was surprised that Helen had paid for a professional makeup job. Jane did not need makeup at all.

"Look Auntie Em," she said wistfully. "Beth is wearing the same dress as me. She looks awesome."

"That dress looks much prettier in aqua," said her aunt in a loud voice. "And it fits you much better because you have a figure like a model." Jane smiled at her aunt. She was sure that Beth had heard her comments.

When Beth walked onto the stage to accept her diploma, the crowd erupted in applause. People hooted and cheered long after she had walked down the steps with her head held high. Jane looked terrified when it was her turn. Her little group of supporters cheered and applauded but was unable to duplicate the thunderous applause that was reserved for the popular students. As she climbed the steps to the stage, someone shouted, "Jane gives BJs," and there was laughter.

After the ceremony, she reluctantly accompanied Trevor Allen to the school dance. He was proud to escort the prettiest girl to the party but Jane believed that he simply felt sorry for her. They had one dance together and ate some pizza then she called her mother to come and drive her home.

10.

Summer

It was a hot day in July when Helen drove a sullen Jane to summer school in Toxteth. "Mom, I wish I hadn't signed up for Learning Strategies," she grumbled. "It was a bad idea. Let's just go home and forget it."

"No, I don't think you should pass up the opportunity of earning a grade nine credit in advance. It will give you a head start and besides, it's only a three week course," said Helen as she stopped in front of the school and gave her daughter a hug. "Good luck," she said. "See you later."

As she walked through the door, Jane was greeted warmly by Monica Johnson, a capricious classmate who never seemed interested in having any girlfriends but rather, concentrated on trying to impress the boys. "Let's sit together in class," she suggested with a friendly gap-toothed grin. Although Jane remembered being bullied by her during the school year, she was willing to forgive and forget if Monica now wanted to be friends.

Taking her seat in the classroom, Jane was pleased to see Trevor Allen sitting across the aisle. She felt encouraged and flattered when he smiled and asked if she would like to join him for lunch later in the cafeteria. Maybe things will get better, she thought, hopefully.

At lunchtime as she waited for Trevor with her bagged lunch in hand, Jane spotted him walking down the hallway chatting with another boy. To her surprise, when the two boys caught sight of her waving to them, they turned on their heels and ran from her. Thinking it was a game, she gave chase, calling Trevor's name, but when she followed them out into the schoolyard, the boys laughed and pelted her with stones. Hurt and confused, she ate her lunch alone in the girl's washroom. Monica, who had witnessed the schoolyard scene, decided that Jane was to be avoided.

"Trevor Allen doesn't like me after all," Jane told her mother during the car ride home, "and Monica Johnson just pretended to be my friend because she thought she could meet boys if she hung out with me. I have no friends at school. Things will never get better."

Finally the weekend arrived and Jane was excited about getting away from Allerton for a couple of days. She had been invited to spend some time in Toronto with Trevor Brown and his family who lived in a small cooperative townhouse.

Helen parked her car in the courtyard and surveyed her surroundings before venturing outside. It looked like a rough neighbourhood. Little children were playing in a puddle of dirty water and a group of teenagers sat languidly on the curb, smoking. "I wonder if they're the drug lords who beat up Trevor last night," Jane commented.

"What?"

"Yeah, Trevor told me last night on MSN. He was on his way to the store for his mom when the drug lords beat him so badly that his nose was broken. Let's go Mom, he's waiting for me," said Jane as she swung the car door open and grabbed her pink backpack.

Helen reluctantly locked the car and followed her daughter. Mrs. Brown had made no mention of Trevor being hurt when they had spoken on the phone that morning. Helen suspected that, like Jane, he had a vivid imagination.

The little townhouse was untidy and smoky but Doreen and Gary Brown seemed like nice people. Gary, a stocky man wearing shorts and an undershirt, sat on a lumpy floral couch smoking a cigarette and watching soccer on television. Doreen smiled and offered tea and cookies. As they sat with Mrs. Brown, Trevor came bounding into the room, grabbed some cookies and said hello. Helen noted that there was not a scratch on him and he certainly did not have a broken nose. After drinking her tea, Helen thanked the Browns, gave Jane a kiss and said goodbye. She believed that it was good for her daughter to be away from Allerton and the computer for a few days, and Trevor seemed to be a harmless young boy. She hoped that she was not making a mistake.

On the sixth of July, Jane was about to walk into Dr. Feldman's office when he pointed to the mat at his door. "Oh I'm sorry," she apologized, "I forgot." Carefully she wiped her shoes on the mat and said goodbye to her mother. Helen went to the hospital cafeteria where she nervously drank coffee and tried to concentrate on a paperback novel.

Dr. Feldman quietly read notes provided to him by Tracey Hogan as Jane waited patiently and glanced at his sandaled feet under the desk. Finally, the doctor looked up and regarded his patient. He asked about eating problems. Jane admitted that she did not like eating in front of people in the school cafeteria. This made her feel nervous and self-conscious. She confessed that she also felt anxious at night and often checked to make sure that the back door and all of the windows were locked. The doctor asked a number of seemingly random questions. Although she enjoyed the attention, Jane did not believe that he would be of any help to her. When asked if she knew how old she had been when she stopped drinking from a baby bottle, she thought it a funny question and replied that she had been seven-years-old.

Helen went through the ritual of wiping her feet on the mat before entering Dr. Feldman's office. It was the eleventh of July and she had taken the day off work to be interviewed alone as part of the assessment process. The doctor enquired about her childhood and she answered honestly. There was not much to tell.

Helen and her older sister, Emily, had lived with their parents, Stephen and Jane Jones, in a small bungalow in Toronto. Their childhood years had been happy and uneventful. When Stephen and Jane retired, they had moved to the Allerton area to provide support for Helen, who by then was a single mother with four children. After the births of six grandsons, they had been delighted to have a granddaughter. Jane Jones passed away in 1997 when her namesake was just five-years-old, and Stephen passed away in 1999.

Helen and her husband Greg Collins had four children before separating in 1992 when Jane was three months old. Greg had visited his children regularly for a number of years after the separation but in 1999, just after her father's death, Helen had requested a formal separation agreement and child support from Greg. His visits stopped. Helen believed that it would have been easier for the children if their father had died, since she could have told them that he was a wonderful person who loved them. Although she did, in fact, tell them that he cared about them in his own way, they suspected that he did not. He had abandoned them. James, who was twenty-two years old, never spoke of his father. Twenty-year-old Joe had no desire to ever see him again, and Chris, seventeen, sometimes said that he felt hurt and rejected by his father. Jane still clung to the hope that she would someday be reunited with her dad.

"How old was Jane when she stopped drinking from a baby bottle?" Dr. Feldman asked.

Helen thought this a bizarre question, but answered, "She was about a year old."

On the twenty-first of July, after she and Jane had wiped their shoes on the mat, Dr. Feldman showed Helen a copy of Jane's assessment, indicating that she was suffering from Obsessive Compulsive Disorder and required a drug called Prozac to calm her nerves. He suggested that she might also have an eating disorder and mentioned that there was an eating disorder clinic at Southern Ontario Hospital. Helen was unsure about the OCD diagnosis but was absolutely certain that her daughter did not have any sort of eating disorder. She simply felt nervous eating in the school cafeteria with the bullies. She ate well at home and had neither anorexia nor bulimia. She explained this to the doctor who advised that the eating disorder program was voluntary and that Jane herself should make the decision. Jane said that she was sure that she did not have an eating disorder or OCD. "If those kids at school would just leave me alone, I would be fine. I would be perfectly normal," she said.

Dr. Feldman warned that mixing non-prescription drugs or alcohol with the Prozac could cause auditory or visual hallucinations. Jane recalled Trevor's description of hallucinations produced by mixing Ritalin with Ecstasy and wondered if he had been telling the truth.

As she and her mother left the doctor's office, they were confronted by Tracey Hogan. Although Tracey seemed surprised, Helen wondered if she had been waiting for them in the hallway. "I think you should come and see me again," Tracy suggested to Jane with a friendly smile.

"She really likes me and wants to be my friend," Jane said to her mother during the drive home to Allerton. "Please make an appointment for me Mom."

On Thursday, the third of August, Jane met privately with Tracey Hogan while Helen sat in the waiting room nervously studying photographs in an old National Geographic magazine. Trevor sat next to her, reading a comic book.

When questioned, Jane told Tracey that Dr. Feldman had prescribed a drug called Prozac to calm her nerves. "He thinks I have OCD and an eating disorder but I know that I don't," she reported.

Tracey then asked about non-prescription drug use and Jane whispered that Trevor had given her a zip-lock bag full of Pot that she had been smoking every day. This was not true, but she thought it sounded impressive. Trevor had, in fact, brought some Pot from Toronto to share with her and she had taken a few puffs but did not like the sensation of smoke going into her lungs.

Jane was not careful when she spoke to Tracey. She talked as though she were chatting with one of her young friends, and often exaggerated. When asked about her appetite, she reported always feeling hungry because there was never anything to eat in the house. By this she meant that there were no handy snack foods to grab, such as cookies, potato chips or chocolate bars. The only foods that her mother had bought required some preparation. Tracey was alarmed. "No food in the house!" she shrieked.

"No," replied Jane, pleased with this reaction. "I haven't eaten since Monday."

It was very encouraging that Tracey treated her as a friend. She believed that her new confidant liked her as a person and enjoyed her company. She definitely wanted to continue the appointments. However, toward the end of the session, when asked about her fears, she was becoming bored and wanted to leave and perhaps go to McDonald's with Trevor and her mother. She provided Tracey with a random list. "I'm afraid of paper, paper cuts, bugs, someone breaking into my house. I'm afraid to go into the bathroom in case there are bugs." Tracey gave her a book entitled *What to Do When You're Scared & Worried* and suggested that she read it with her mother. Jane felt insulted since the book was obviously written for a young child and no girl her age would read a book with her mother.

When Helen later joined them, she advised Tracey that Dr. Feldman had prescribed a mild anti-depressant for her daughter. At the mention of the doctor's name, Jane remarked that he always wore sandals. Tracey then commented that he was indeed a "strange duck" who had expressed his opinion on her hair style. Jane laughed and glanced at her mother, who was not smiling. Helen was surprised that a hospital counsellor would make such a disrespectful comment about a doctor. It seemed very unprofessional. Tracey recommended another session and an appointment was made for August 14th.

Eleven days later, on Monday, August 14th, Jane was back at Southern Ontario Hospital in Tracey's office. She worried that she did not have anything entertaining to report but was pleased that she had brought Trevor's burned medication bottle to show Tracey. She had no idea why he had set fire to his empty Ritalin bottle but hoped that it would elicit a shocked response. Trevor often did strange things that she found intriguing. She decided that he was an interesting topic of conversation and explained to Tracey that she had never known anyone like him. He was different from the kids she knew in Allerton and Toxteth. She confided that he lived in a scary neighbourhood in Toronto and sometimes hit her when they were alone. She disclosed that, although he was only thirteen, he was a big boy and she was sometimes afraid of him. He had once chased her with his Insulin syringe. She confessed that he had introduced her to a drug called Ecstasy and she had been experimenting with it in the hope that she might not feel so depressed and worried about school.

"Are you still having suicidal thoughts?" asked Tracey.

"Yes, whenever Trevor hits me for no reason. He hurts my feelings and I feel bad about myself."

"So, is your relationship with Trevor not going well?"

"When he is mean and tries to scare me, I really feel like killing him."

"How did you get those scratches on your arms?"

"Oh, I was playing in the park and scratched them on the trees."

Tracey pursed her lips. Jane was sometimes disconcerted by her friend's lack of ability to distinguish fact from fiction.

When she spoke to Tracey, her guard was always down. She believed her to be a friend with whom she could talk freely, just as she did with her young girlfriends. She recalled that her mother had been angry with her because, like other teenagers, her bedroom was a mess. She had been too lazy to pick up pop cans, candy wrappers and such and was in the habit of just throwing them under her bed. She told Tracey that she had been doing this, and that the state of her bedroom made her mom angry.

Tracey noted: *"Collecting garbage in her room, hides stuff under things, paper, wrappers, cans."*

Jane was pleased that an adult was interested in every little detail of her life. In an effort to be more entertaining, she repeated stories that Trevor had told her, but attributed the behaviour to herself. She produced his burned medication bottle, claiming it to be her own.

Tracey wrote: *"Broke into a car, stole a number of items. Has been starting fires for a long time and burns paper, toys books, self. Burnt self yesterday, and medication bottle."*

When asked the usual question about her fears, Jane said that she feared strangers and sometimes felt that people were staring at her, talking about her or even laughing at her. Tracey did not understand that she was simply over-dramatizing normal teenage feelings of self-consciousness. Untrained and inexperienced, she misconstrued what had been said and believed it to be indicative of a mental disorder.

Next on Tracey's agenda was the bullying issue. It had been weeks since graduation and Jane had been trying to forget the bullying. Tracey reminded her of her plan to kill the bullies and asked if she had given it any more thought. Jane considered this idea for a moment then remembered her favourite movie, *The Nightmare Before Christmas*. She recalled that Santa Claus had been kidnapped and taken to Halloween Town where he was tortured by a boogeyman, and she remembered Sally, the doll with the stitched face.

"The plan would be to kidnap Beth from her house in Toxteth," said Jane. "Then I would take her to a wooded area in Allerton." She was imagining Halloween Town. "There, I would slit the corners of her mouth from ear to ear and then sew it back up," she said with a grin. She was thinking of Sally, and expected Tracey to laugh, but she did not. She looked horrified.

"Then what would you do?" she asked, wide eyed.

"Oh, I guess I would probably torture her," sighed Jane. She was finding this conversation to be very therapeutic.

Although Tracey had an odd expression on her face, it did not occur to Jane that she might actually believe this story. She presumed her to be playing along with the fantasy as part of the therapy process.

"Would you kill her?" asked Tracey.

"Yeah, maybe beat, hang or electrocute her. She deserves to feel pain because she ruined my life."

"What would you do to avoid getting caught?"

"I guess I would have to kill myself. Then I would get married under the big tree." She was thinking of another animated Tim Burton movie called *Corpse Bride*.

Tracey did not stop to consider that this plan made no sense. Although she knew that it was eighteen kilometres from Allerton to Toxteth, she did not ask Jane how she planned to make the trip from Allerton to Toxteth and then return to a wooded area of Allerton while holding Beth at knifepoint. She did not ask how a small girl like Jane could overpower Beth and her family. And, she did not ask where this idea had come from. She simply asked Jane if she knew where Beth lived.

"And do you plan to kill anyone else?" Tracey wondered.

"Oh, maybe Trevor Allen if he gives me a hard time," responded Jane offhandedly, "and maybe Monica. Well, maybe I wouldn't kill Monica." She was becoming bored and gave little thought to what she was saying.

Tracey made a note that Jane had divulged a plan to kill Beth Henderson and was considering killing her boyfriend, Trevor, and possibly Monica. At the end of the session, when Helen joined them, she made no mention of what Jane had said, but suggested they meet on Friday the 18th since she would soon be off on vacation. Helen advised her that she and Jane would also be going on a holiday the following week.

It was Wednesday afternoon and, except for the three pets, Jane was alone in the house. She logged onto MSN and found that Nadia had changed her name to xxxglam.

| Session Start: Wednesday, August 16, 2006
| Participants:
| sallythedoll
| xxxglam

[04:01:10 PM] xxxglam: why would you get tim to add me you disgusting bitch

[04:01:28 PM] sallythedoll: he asked for it. why would you add my msn again

[04:01:57 PM] xxxglam: haha it was on my old contact list so it just added you. I don't even like you or want to talk to you. You're like 12

[04:02:12 PM] sallythedoll: 14

[04:02:15 PM] xxxglam: and you're a slut, a nasty, greasy, slut

[04:02:40 PM] sallythedoll: haha get a life. Honestly you're dissing someone you DON'T even know. thats pretty sad

[04:02:57 PM] xxxglam: lol

[04:03:36 PM] sallythedoll: hmm I didn't do anything to you, yet you're dissing me, do you think you're cool when you do it or something? GET A LIFE loser

[04:03:49 PM] xxxglam: i'm far from a loser and thats why i'm telling you that I hate you so fucking much

[04:04:02 PM] sallythedoll: you're the loser dissing people you don't even know i don't care if you hate me why would i WANT to know someone like you

[04:04:21 PM] xxxglam: haha when i see you at school i'm punching you and literally

[04:04:58 PM] sallythedoll: so go ahead and punch me big girl

[04:05:00 PM] xxxglam: you're just a try hard wanna be scene kid. I think your disgusting

[04:05:22 PM] sallythedoll: do you think that punching someone you don't know makes you cool

[04:05:39 PM] xxxglam: you were with that greasy haired loser guy and thats why we spit on you at school. you're a skinny ugly girl with no friends. i've got a boyfriend. i'm popular

[04:06:01 PM] sallythedoll: if you have SOOOO many friends then why are you on MSN dissing me? someone with tons of friends wouldn't do that. they wouldn't care about someone like me. look whose little miss popular now

[04:06:56 PM] xxxglam: that's right i am popular i actually have people here and we are planning our night out online but you wouldn't know that because you just make assumptions. thats all you can do and that's all you ever will do because you're trashy

[04:07:12 PM] sallythedoll: oh no what a diss ^ o)

[04:07:27 PM] xxxglam: i hate you so much. i've never had so much hate for someone i didn't know before. and you're a thief, you stole from beth who was supposed to be your friend

[04:07:46 PM] sallythedoll: what would i steal from beth?

[04:07:58 PM] xxxglam: your just low class and everyone hates you. i'm going to smash your face in

[04:08:06 PM] sallythedoll: uh huh?

[04:08:08 PM] xxxglam: you afraid?

[04:08:15 PM] sallythedoll: get a life. you're DISSING someone you DON'T know. WHO does that?

[04:08:24 PM] xxxglam: i know about you and i don't like what i've heard

[04:08:27 PM] sallythedoll: lies?

[04:08:30 PM] xxxglam: i just hate you

[04:08:34 PM] sallythedoll: good. THEN SHUT UP. POINT PROVEN. GO AWAY. DONT TALK TO ME ON MSN OR ANYWHERE

[04:08:43 PM] xxxglam: school is soon. are you excited? i am

When Helen arrived home from work, Jane was sitting at the computer trembling as she stared at a blank screen. She was silent during dinner and would not say what was troubling her. After dinner, she put the dirty dishes into the dishwasher, had a shower and went to bed at seven o'clock.

Whenever anyone in the family had a computer problem, Chris was usually able to solve it. He had taken some Information Technology courses and was affectionately known as a "computer nerd." With this in mind Helen approached her son for help. She told him that she suspected his sister was being bullied on MSN and asked if he could access the conversations.

"Sure Mom," he said. "No problem."

Chris was able to access all of Jane's MSN conversations from the months of June through August. He printed them and gave the hard copies to his mother.

While driving to Southern Ontario Hospital on Friday, August 18th, Helen gave Jane the copies of the MSN conversations. "Chris printed these for us," she said. "I think you should show them to Tracey. Maybe she will be able to suggest some coping strategies for you."

Jane grinned at her mother. "Chris is so cool," she said with pride.

Relieved that she was able to provide solid evidence of the abuse she had endured, Jane handed the copies to Tracey as soon as she walked into her office. Tracey found the conversations somewhat confusing but understood them well enough to know that Jane had been telling the truth about being victimized by other girls. She put them aside for later discussion when Helen joined them at the end of the session.

Jane talked about Trevor, with whom she had spent many days that summer. He was a funny boy with a wild imagination. She again related his stories of breaking into cars and stealing things, about setting fires and doing drugs, but did not mention the drug lords. Although she enjoyed his company, Jane said that she was looking forward to getting away from everything and seeing new places on a driving holiday with her mom, aunt, uncle and cousins, Mark and Stephen. She had never been out of the province of Ontario and the trip to Quebec and New York State would be awesome.

Tracey, as she had at every session, prodded her about the plan to kill Beth Henderson. It seemed to Jane that Tracey did not want her to forget about the bullying and move forward with her life. She was becoming tired of this subject but wanted so much to please her friend that she repeated her *Nightmare Before Christmas* plan to kidnap Beth. In reality, she just wanted to forgive and forget but had the impression that Tracey would be disappointed if she confessed to wanting to be friends with Beth when school resumed in September.

When Helen joined them at the end of the session, Tracey asked Jane about the other girl involved in the MSN conversations. "She's a mean girl named Nadia Reeves," responded Jane. "She's older than Beth and me and is really strange. I don't even know her and I don't know why she hates me. I think Beth must have told her lies about me. I just want her to leave me alone."

"Oh I know her. She has a history of bullying," said Tracey with a smile. "She also comes here for counselling. She has been skipping school and the Children's Aid Society has been involved with her family. Her social worker's name is Rita. She has many issues and has been involved with Kinark Child and

Family Services." Tracey smiled conspiratorially. "Don't tell anyone that I told you this," she whispered. "I could get into trouble for telling you about Nadia." Then, in the presence of Jane and Helen, she made a phone call to Nadia's social worker. Since Rita was unavailable, she left a voice message.

Jane smiled at Tracey. She truly believed that she had a friend. Helen felt worried and uncomfortable that Tracey had so cavalierly divulged confidential patient information about another of her young clients. She had grave concerns about the safety of her daughter's private health information and considered lodging a complaint against Tracey.

"Mrs. Collins, I wonder if I might keep these copies of the MSN conversations," said Tracey. "I want to fax them to a friend of mine who is on the police force. Perhaps Nadia should be charged with uttering threats to Jane."

Jane felt overjoyed that she finally had a friend who was definitely on her side. Not only had Tracey provided her with secret information about Nadia, but she was also going to arrange to have Nadia punished for being a bully.

An appointment was made for August 28th and Tracey provided a reminder card. As Helen was about to follow her daughter out of the office, Tracey tapped her on the shoulder. "If you have any problems with Jane while I'm on vacation, you can call this phone number and have her admitted to Youthdale," she whispered. She took the appointment card from Helen and wrote "Youthdale" and a phone number on the back, but did not explain what sort of place it was, nor did Helen think to ask. She was mystified and could not imagine why she would do such a thing.

After they had left her office, Tracey hurriedly made some notes and then requested a meeting with Dr. Feldman. She expressed her concerns to him that Jane was completely out of control and had a homicidal plan to kill people. Dr. Feldman was a psychiatrist who understood his young patient. He assured Tracey that Jane was not capable of carrying out any such a plan.

11.

Vacation

Emily and Jack Morrison had been taking their three boys on summer driving holidays for a number of years. In 1999, at age nineteen, their oldest son, Adam, had stopped going on these trips and the Morrisons began inviting their nephew Chris to join them as company for Mark. Their middle son, Stephen, had many challenges. He was unable to speak and struggled with deafness, autism and poor vision. He communicated through supported typing on an alphabet board.

For the next few years, the family, including Chris, travelled across Canada and the United States each summer and the two younger boys became close friends. However, as teenagers, they grew apart and Mark began spending more time with Jane.

The summer of 2006 was a turning point in the lives of Mark and his parents. It was early in July when, at age sixteen, he had come out to his family as being gay. This came as a complete surprise to Emily and Jack since there had been no obvious indications during his childhood or early teen years. He had always been athletic, like his brother Adam, and played baseball, soccer and hockey. His closest friends were straight boys and he had been a Cub Scout. He enjoyed violent, male oriented video games, as did Chris. Tall, blond and handsome, he was popular with girls. Recently, he had met his boyfriend, Jason, through a girlfriend from school. Fortunately, he seemed happy, well-adjusted and self-confident.

Although dazed and somewhat disoriented, Emily and Jack made an effort to hide their fears from Mark. They had always worried about Stephen's future because he had severe disabilities and would never be independent. Now, suddenly, they were also concerned about Mark's future. Thoughts of discrimination, lack of equal rights, hate crimes against gay people, the spectre of AIDS, and a host of other fears troubled them as they prepared for a family holiday. Emily decided to join PFLAG, a support group for parents of gay, lesbian, bisexual and transgender people, upon her return from the vacation.

On Sunday, the twentieth of August, Helen and Jane climbed into the Morrison family van and the group of six was off on a trip to Quebec and New York State. Jack drove as Helen followed their progress on a map and Emily sat next to Stephen who made happy clucking noises as he played with a slinky. Jane and Mark shared the back seat, listening to music on their ipods, and throughout the journey, Mark sent frequent text messages to Jason.

Everyone loved Montreal, especially Jane. Helen bought her daughter a "J'aime Montréal" T-shirt in a little shop on St. Catherine Street and Jane wore it proudly for the rest of the day. She, Mark and Stephen lit candles in Notre Dame Cathedral in memory of their grandparents and then the family took a calèche ride through old Montreal. The friendly driver, Guillaume, introduced himself and his horse, Nordique. "Poor Nordique works too hard," commented Jane as she patted his nose afterward.

"Smile," said Emily as she snapped a photo of Jane and Nordique.

Later, as they dined at Les Pyrénées Restaurant, Jane sat beside her cousin Stephen and held his alphabet board to help him order food. He spelled "CHICKEN NUGGETS AND FRIES."

"Stephen and I want to go to McDonald's," she said.

Later that evening, the family drove to the top of Mount Royal to view the beautiful city at night and Uncle Jack gave Stephen, Mark and Jane a brief history of former Prime Minister, Pierre Trudeau who had lived in Montreal.

In New York State, the family stopped to admire the beauty of the Ausable Chasm in the Adirondack Mountains. Typical teens, Jane and Mark were not quite as interested in the natural beauty of the canyon as was the rest of the group. "Look at that," said Uncle Jack. "When Samuel de Champlain first explored this area four hundred years ago, it looked just as it does today!"

"It's breathtaking!" exclaimed Emily. Helen agreed.

"Um hmm. Can we go now?" asked Mark.

The van headed down through New York State and pulled in at the Kon Tiki Hotel at Lake George. Immediately, Jane and Mark changed into their bathing suits and jumped into the heated pool. "This is more like it," said Mark. Jack and Stephen also went for a swim. Emily and Helen went shopping.

The following day, while the others enjoyed a leisurely paddlewheel cruise on Lake George, Mark and Jane had fun just being kids at "The Great Escape," a "Six Flags" theme park. There they went on roller coaster rides and ate cotton candy. Later that evening, after a Hawaiian theme dinner in the hotel restaurant, the family walked through the little town of Lake George where Jane and Mark spotted "Dr. Morbid's Haunted House." After their Haunted House experience, Emily took a photo of the Frankenstein monster with his arms around the two of them.

As they drove home at the end of the holiday, Mark slept in the back seat while Jane sat with Stephen who waved his hands in the air uncontrollably and made loud throaty noises. He had lost his slinky and needed something to calm him. Although he was a bright young man, Stephen often had difficulty controlling his body due to autism. Jane took the elastic band from her ponytail and handed it to him while Emily held up his alphabet board. Stephen typed "THANKS JANE THIS WILL HELP," then began twirling the band back and forth between his thumb and index finger. The throaty noises stopped and he fell asleep.

The van pulled into Helen's driveway and she and Jane wearily climbed out. Mark carried their suitcases into the house, then waved goodbye to his parents and brother. His aunt had promised to pick up Jason the following day on the way to Jane's appointment with Dr. Feldman. As he helped Jane and her mother put a load of laundry into the washing machine, he suggested renting a movie at Blockbuster for the evening's entertainment, but Jane decided to go for a bike ride instead. "I need some exercise. I've been sitting in the van for too long," she said.

The escape from reality was over and Jane began to worry about the upcoming school year and the bullies. She hopped on her bike and rode over to the park where she smelled a familiar aroma. A boy whom she recognized as Kyle Weston from school, stood among the trees. When he offered her a joint, she accepted, forgetting Dr. Feldman's warning about mixing drugs with the Prozac that he had prescribed for her. She wanted to be happy like Kyle who was giggling for no apparent reason. After taking a few drags, she began to feel disoriented and unable to determine if the whispering voices she heard were emanating from shadowy figures standing among the trees or her own mind. Frightened, she grabbed her bike and raced home. As she walked in the door, her mother immediately recognized the odour in her hair and clothing.

"What is wrong with you?" she screamed furiously, "You come back from a nice holiday and start smoking pot! Where did it come from? Who gave it to you? I don't understand you!"

"You shut up and leave me alone!" Jane shouted as she slammed her bedroom door.

Mark, who had been sitting in the living room watching a Batman movie and eating popcorn, was oblivious to the drama unfolding in the house.

The following day, August 25th, Helen stopped in the town of Waverly and picked up Jason, a friendly, dark-haired teenager with a quiet demeanor. As the two boys chatted happily in the back seat, Helen and Jane drove in silence to Southern Ontario Hospital.

Jane wiped her feet on the mat and, gesturing toward her mother, shouted to Dr. Feldman, "Does she have to be here?"

"Yes she does," he answered sternly. "Why are you angry with your mother?"

"She's giving me a hard time just because I smoked a little pot."

The doctor raised his bushy eyebrows. "I warned you about taking drugs with the Prozac. Did you forget?"

Jane tried to explain her frightening experience to the doctor but had difficulty expressing herself. "I kind of went crazy and heard weird voices and stuff. I saw shadows of people who weren't really there. It was very scary."

Dr. Feldman was not at all sympathetic. "Don't exaggerate," he said with a laugh. "You're making far too much of nothing. Just don't do it again." At the conclusion of this appointment, he increased the dosage of Prozac and made a follow-up appointment for September 29th.

When they met Mark and Jason, who had been waiting patiently outside the doctor's office, Helen suggested lunch at Swiss Chalet Restaurant. As the foursome walked out into the warm August air, Jane smiled and Jason looked relieved. "I hate being inside hospitals," he said. "They creep me out."

12.

I Would Just Walk Away

Helen received an email from Greg. It was a little note mentioning that he had been having some minor health problems. He wrote as though they had not been estranged for the past seven years. Helen wondered why on earth he would think she cared about his health. Under normal circumstances she would have ignored this intrusion into her life, but lately she had been feeling so lonely and worried about Jane that she responded. She told him that their daughter had been bullied at school and was seeing a counsellor and a psychiatrist at the hospital. To her surprise Greg suggested that Jane spend the Labour Day weekend with him in Toronto. Although Jane had not seen her father since the age of seven, Helen agreed that it might be good for her to reconnect with him. Allowing her daughter to spend the weekend in Toronto with Greg was a decision that would haunt Helen for the rest of her life.

In the meantime, Jane missed her friend Trevor and wondered if he too was feeling anxious about school. Helen agreed to a two day visit and met Trevor and his mother at the Newton Mall. When Trevor climbed into her car on August 26th, he was carrying Ecstasy and Marijuana in his backpack to share with Jane.

On Monday, the 28th of August, Helen, Jane and Trevor drove to Southern Ontario Hospital for an appointment with Tracey Hogan. "I don't really have anything to talk to Tracey about today," sighed Jane as they pulled into the hospital parking lot. "I'll have to think of something interesting."

While Jane met privately with Tracey, Trevor sat in the waiting room with Helen and tried to engage her in his stories of being hunted by drug lords. "I'm afraid they know where I live so we'll probably have to move," he said.

Helen smiled at the boy. "Trevor, why don't you look at one of the magazines over there," she suggested. He looked briefly at the magazines then found a toy tractor to play with.

Jane was in a happy mood when she walked into Tracey's office. She had just returned from a great holiday with her cousins, Trevor was treating her well, and best of all, she would be seeing her dad the following weekend. However, when Tracey asked how she had been, Jane admitted that Trevor had brought some Pot and Ecstasy from Toronto to share with her. She explained that she had taken these drugs in the hope that they would help her to feel less anxious about the upcoming school year.

"I'm afraid to go to school because things might be as bad as they were last year," she said.

"What will you do if you see Beth at school on Tuesday?" asked Tracey.

"I don't know," Jane responded slowly. "She said on MSN that she wants to be my friend, but I'm not sure that I trust her."

Now, at this point, a competent counsellor might have realized that Jane was simply asking permission to forgive Beth and move forward with her life. This thought did not occur to Tracey.

"Do you plan to harm Beth?" she asked.

"No, not if she doesn't bug me."

"But suppose she does?"

"Then I would punch her in the face."

"Would you really do that Jane?"

"No, I would just walk away."

"What about your plan? Do you think you might follow through with it?"

"Maybe."

After talking with Jane, Tracey called Helen into her office to answer some questions.

"Has Jane been having any eating problems?"

"No. I've explained to her that the Prozac must be taken with meals to avoid stomach upset."

"Are you going to continue the appointments with Dr. Feldman?"

"Well, Jane doesn't really need a psychiatrist but she will be going for a follow-up appointment in September, only because she is taking Prozac for her nerves. If all goes well at school, the medication may be unnecessary."

"Are you aware of Jane's plan to harm her classmate?"

"I know my daughter. Jane may say that she is going to hurt someone, but she would never do it. She knows that if she were to hurt Beth, then Beth would be seen as the victim when all along she has been the bully. Jane is a very passive girl and has never hurt anyone in her life. I am concerned about the bullying though. Do you think it would be a good idea for Jane to switch schools and go to Allerton High School in September?"

"Absolutely not! Switching schools would be a big mistake Mrs. Collins!" insisted Tracey emphatically. She then gave Helen an appointment card for September 5th at 3:00 p.m. and, turning to Jane, said, "Good luck on your first day of school. You can leave a little early that day to come and see me."

However, unbeknownst to either of them, Jane and Helen were never to set foot in Tracey's office again.

13.

That Guy

Helen had arranged to meet Greg at the Newton train station on Thursday evening. She was assigned to work in Youth Court that day and, in order to avoid having to return home before meeting him, brought Jane to the courthouse with her. Jane had recently plucked up the courage to have her ear pierced and proudly wore a new earring. All of the trendy kids had them. The clerks at the courthouse admired the earring and made her feel welcome. She felt privileged and important when they took her behind the scenes to meet one of the judges, but very sorry for the troubled young people who had been charged with offenses. She could only imagine how frightened they must feel.

It had been years since Helen had seen Greg. As she and Jane drove to the train station to meet him, she tried to recall why she had married him so long ago. She remembered being captivated by his charm the first time she had seen him, a bearded young folk singer performing in a coffee house. Her parents and sister had not been impressed when they first met him one fateful Christmas day. He had become so obnoxious after drinking a few beers that Helen's father, Stephen, had been on the verge of ordering him to leave. Jane Jones had worried that her daughter was about to make the biggest mistake of her life.

Although Greg had not been a model husband or father, Helen felt certain that he would not harm his daughter. He was a mild-mannered, non-violent man who loved to play the guitar and piano, as did Jane.

A middle-aged man approached Helen and Jane, smiled and commented on how pretty they both looked. Helen could not believe that the strange looking man standing before her was Greg, her former husband. His eyes were unrecognizable, there were marionette lines around his mouth and his gray-streaked red hair was combed forward from the crown of his head, giving him an odd appearance. He was beardless.

"Is that him Mom?" whispered Jane. "He looks like a turtle when he smiles."

Greg drove his daughter to the west end of Toronto where he lived in a shabby apartment over his place of work, an Italian Restaurant. He and Jane ate pizza in the restaurant and he proudly introduced her to his boss, Tony, and other staff members. Charmed, Tony patted Jane's head and gave her a fifty dollar bill. Greg had mentioned to his co-workers that he was a father, but no one had actually believed him. All were surprised to see that he did indeed have a daughter.

When Jane saw her father's apartment, she had second thoughts about spending the weekend. There was a layer of greasy dust on the stove in the kitchen and crumbs covered the counter top. The fridge smelled of sour milk and contained nothing but bottles of beer. She wondered if there might be mice under the scummy sink. There were stains and cigarette burns on the carpet, and the bed sheets looked ancient and dirty. Greg pointed to an old roll-away bed with a thin mattress and told his daughter that a stripper had slept there. He then asked if she would prefer to sleep with him at night. Jane declined the offer, saying that she would sleep alone in the stripper's bed. She was becoming alarmed but decided to give him a chance before calling her mother. She excused his behaviour, hoping that he was simply inept and unpracticed at being with young people. She desperately wanted Greg to be a loving dad like those of the girls at school.

"We'll go sightseeing around Toronto tomorrow," promised Greg.

Jane brightened. "That would be cool, Dad!"

The following day, Greg, camera in hand, took his daughter around the city and showed her the sights. He snapped a photo of her standing in front of city hall. "You look pretty in this picture," he said. "Your boobs look big."

Jane knew that this was not something a normal dad would say to his daughter. Shocked and disappointed, she tried not to cry.

On Saturday evening, after they had eaten an Italian meal and Greg had drunk a few beers, he hit Jane in the groin while demonstrating martial arts and then proceeded to rub the area, ostensibly to ease the pain.

"Don't do that, I'm okay," said Jane, who by now, was genuinely frightened. To her surprise, Greg offered her a beer.

"No thanks, I'm only fourteen. I don't drink real beer, just Root Beer and Coke."

"Would you like me to buy you some pop? There's a convenience store across the street. Do you smoke? I could buy you a pack of smokes too if you like," he offered.

"No thanks. I don't smoke. I would like a Coke though," she responded, hoping that he would leave.

As soon as Greg was out of sight, Jane phoned home and left a message that she wanted to be picked up as soon as possible.

"I'm scared Mom. I want to come home. That guy scares me."

Jane never again referred to Greg as her dad. He was simply "that guy."

14.

Shock

Early Friday morning, Joe was jolted awake by the loud buzz of the doorbell. Glancing at the clock on his night table he was relieved to see that it was only 9:30 in the morning so he rolled over and pulled the covers over his head. Then, a large fist pounded on the door. Angrily, he pulled on his pants and went to investigate.

In the doorway stood two hefty police officers. One of them introduced himself as Detective Bob Rutledge.

"I am looking for Jane Collins," he said. "Is she home?"

Joe smiled, assuming that the detective wanted to speak to his sister about the bullying she had endured during the past few months. He had a keen interest in law enforcement and was hoping to become a police officer himself one day. "No Officer," he answered respectfully. "My sister is in Toronto visiting our father for the weekend. It's kind of strange," he volunteered. "We haven't heard from him in about seven years."

"Is that a fact," said Detective Rutledge as he made a note in his book, then demanded Joe's full name and that of his father and mother. "Have your mother call B District as soon as possible," he ordered, thrusting a contact card at Joe.

After work, Helen arrived home to three pets and an otherwise empty house. As a single mother of four children, this would normally be a treat since dinner was now optional and she had the luxury of reading the newspaper uninterrupted. But the silence seemed eerie. She spotted a card on the kitchen table with the name Detective Bob Rutledge printed on it and a note from Joe. Assuming that Tracey Hogan must have faxed the MSN information to her friend in the police department, and wondering if charges might be laid against Nadia, she phoned B District only to be advised that Detective Rutledge was unavailable.

Helen had volunteered to work in WASH (weekend and statutory holidays) court on Saturday, the second of September, because it meant extra money. During her coffee break, she was finally able to reach the detective.

"Hello Detective Rutledge, My name is Helen Collins. My son tells me that you were looking for my daughter, Jane, yesterday."

"That's right Mrs. Collins. It was in connection with an incident reported by Tracey Hogan, a counsellor at Southern Ontario Hospital."

"Oh yes, my daughter was being bullied at school and on MSN."

"No Mrs. Collins. Your daughter will be arrested and charged with Utter Threat."

"No Detective, you don't understand. My daughter was the victim. She didn't bully anyone."

"I'm not talking about bullying Mrs. Collins. Your daughter uttered a threat to Tracey Hogan to cause death to Beth Henderson. We will be coming to your home or her father's residence to arrest her. I understand that she is currently in Toronto. Please provide me with her father's address."

Helen was dumbfounded. Her head swam and she had difficulty breathing.

"Oh, please don't spoil her weekend with her father. It's the first time she has seen him in years."

"Well, alright. Since she is in Toronto, I guess she isn't a threat to anyone. But I need you to bring her to B District between eleven and midnight Sunday to be arrested."

"What? Are you kidding? No, I won't do that. It would mean that she would be held in jail overnight." This can't be happening, she thought.

"Listen Mrs. Collins, I am bending over backwards to help you. How about bringing her in at 7:00 a.m. on Monday morning? Then after her arrest, she can be processed and proceed to her bail hearing."

"You can't be serious!"

"Listen to me, Mrs. Collins. Bring her in on Monday morning. I won't be available so ask for Detective Young. She will be processed and transported to the courthouse for a bail hearing." With that, he hung up.

Helen phoned her sister in tears and explained what had happened. Jack and Emily spent the evening in Allerton consoling Helen. They were all certain that this misunderstanding would be cleared up and Jane would be able to start school on Tuesday.

Early Sunday morning Greg drove to Newton with Jane and she was reunited with her mother. As soon as he pulled out of the parking lot, she threw her arms around Helen and began to weep. "I don't have a dad after all," she cried. "I never want to see that guy again. I really need to speak to Tracey about my weekend. It was so horrible!"

"It's all my fault," said Helen in abject misery. "I should never have let you go. I am so sorry sweetheart."

Helen did not drive home to Allerton. She and Jane went to Toronto to see Emily and Jack. When they arrived, Jane hugged them both tightly and began to cry again. "I've had the worst weekend of my life," she sobbed.

Emily, Jack and Helen looked at one another. They knew that Jane's weekend was about to get much worse and tried to explain to her that there had been a grave misunderstanding and, as a result, she was to be arrested.

"Don't worry Jane," said Uncle Jack. "Everything will be fine."

On Monday, September the fourth, Helen Collins took her daughter to B District to be arrested and processed. She felt as though her heart had been torn from her chest. It was difficult to breathe. She agonized over the mistake of taking her daughter to Southern Ontario Hospital for help. Why on earth had she trusted Tracey Hogan? She reproached herself for not realizing that the woman was dangerous and certainly not qualified to counsel young people. Jane sat beside her mother crying and trembling uncontrollably. "I thought Tracey liked me," she said between sobs. "I trusted her. I thought she was my friend. Why did she do this to me? She must have hated me all along, just like everyone else."

A police officer read the charge to Jane: "Jane Collins, date of birth – 20 April 1992, a young person within the meaning of the Youth Criminal Justice Act. Between 13 August 2006 and 29 August 2006 at the Town of Newton in the Province of Ontario did knowingly utter a threat to Tracey Hogan to cause death to Beth Henderson contrary to the Criminal Code section 264.1(1) (a)." She looked at him in disbelief.

A female police officer ordered Jane to remove her shoe-laces and her bra because it had underwire. Then she yanked the new earring out of her ear with a pair of pliers and threw it away. Jane was then handcuffed and taken in a police cruiser to bail court. As Helen followed in her car she could see her small daughter seated in the back of the cruiser. She had trouble breathing and felt a heavy weight on her chest as she imagined how frightened Jane must be feeling. So shaky was Helen that she feared she might pass out behind the wheel. This cannot be happening, she thought.

The police cruiser parked at the prisoner's entrance behind the courthouse and Jane was escorted into a small holding cell to await her bail hearing.

Helen parked her car. She was feeling ambivalent about this horrible misunderstanding happening on a holiday weekend. As a private person who did not want her co-workers to know her personal business, she was relieved that few of them would be in the courthouse that day. However, since she could not retain a lawyer during the holiday, she had the choice of either relying on Duty Counsel or having Jane held overnight in jail.

It had been Helen's experience, in her many years as a court reporter, that very few people were denied bail. She had witnessed every type of accused: drunk drivers, wife beaters, even murderers, being granted bail. Often they were released into the custody of less than upstanding citizens. Surely a fourteen-year-old girl with no criminal record, who had done nothing wrong, would be released into the custody of her mother, a court employee. Helen decided that it made sense to rely on Duty Counsel. She promised to treat Jane to lunch at Boston Pizza afterward, so confident was she that there would be no problem.

Walking into the courtroom, she recognized a number of people. Seeing the friendly faces of clerks, Norma and Wendy and court reporter, Marianne, she began to cry. Marianne disappeared and returned with a coffee and a muffin for Helen, and the three women tried to comfort their friend. "Mike Rivers is here today," said Norma. "He's a good lawyer, why don't you ask his advice," she suggested.

When Helen saw that Janet Hale was to be Duty Counsel representing Jane, her heart sank. The woman had a reputation of being lazy and uncaring. Helen was also disappointed that the Justice of the Peace was a young woman known as H. N. L. Woods. She was aware that this JP was not popular among those who worked in the courthouse.

"Are you planning to go and speak to the prisoners?" H. N. L. Woods asked Janet Hale.

"I guess so," replied Ms. Hale. Reluctantly she visited Jane, who was locked in a holding cell.

"Well," said Ms. Hale, as she regarded the frightened girl, "you will either be spending tonight in a hospital bed or a jail cell." Then she waddled out of the bleak little cell.

Mike Rivers' case was to be heard first and then videos of other courts were to be shown. Helen stopped him outside the courtroom and briefly explained what had happened. His face grew red with rage. "She was just a kid venting her feelings to a counsellor," he said angrily. "If I weren't so busy I would help you, Helen. But take my advice and have this thing put over until tomorrow when you can get a good lawyer. Don't trust Hale and Woods with it."

"But that would mean Jane spending the night in jail and missing the first day of school," said Helen.

Then, as Mike rushed off, Janet Hale came shuffling down the hallway. "You should put this over until tomorrow," she said.

"No!" Helen shouted emphatically, "I want this to go forward. I'm taking my daughter home today!"

Helen's head was reeling and her stomach churned as she took her seat in the courtroom behind the Crown Counsel, Natalie Coughlin. She had chatted with Natalie and bought her a coffee the previous week. Natalie turned around briefly and regarded Helen. "Oh, I didn't know this was your daughter," she said.

Seated next to Natalie was a large muscular man wearing a dark suit. He appeared to have no neck and looked as though his large, bullet-shaped head had been shoved down into his shoulders. Helen stared at the fat crease on the back of his shaved head. He turned around and introduced himself as Detective Bob Rutledge from B District. "It is my duty to protect the state," he announced. Helen's eyes widened. From my Jane, she thought.

"There is a detention order on your daughter," he said.

To her horror, Helen looked at the courtroom video monitor and saw her terrified daughter, handcuffed and standing in a dismal holding cell. "Raise your hand if you can hear us," she was instructed. Jane raised both small hands since they were cuffed together.

Then, Natalie Coughlin stood and read the "horrific allegations." She told the court that Jane Collins had devised a diabolical plan to kidnap Beth Henderson at knifepoint, cut her mouth from ear to ear, stitch it back up, then torture and kill her in a wooded area of Allerton. These shocking details had been reported to the police by one Tracey Hogan, a counsellor at Southern Ontario Hospital.

Detective Bob Rutledge was asked to take the stand. Helen had never, in all her years as a court reporter, seen allegations provided in this manner at a bail hearing. The Detective had interviewed Tracey Hogan at the hospital and she had stated that on August 14th, Jane had divulged her plan to abduct torture and kill Beth Henderson in September. Tracey had described Jane as being a small, slim fourteen-year-old who abused drugs on a daily basis and was in the habit of lighting fires in her home. The Detective had determined the identity of the intended "victim" by questioning Mr. Mario Monardo, the Principal of St. Joan of Arc Catholic School. He had then proceeded to interview Beth Henderson at her home in Toxteth. He stated that he had received the following information from Beth Henderson:

- Nadia bullied Jane, I never did;
- Jane didn't have any real friends;
- She copied other people – clothes and behaviour;
- She started being weird and became friends with others;
- Last saw her at grade 8 grad;
- Jane never threatened me;
- Everything seemed okay between us.

Helen was livid. Her head pounded and she broke out in a cold sweat as she considered the betrayal. Her daughter's confidential health information, that should have been protected by the hospital, had been shared with, not only the police, but the Henderson family and Mr. Monardo, the school principal. She wondered why the police had not interviewed Jane herself before arresting her and charging her with a crime. And why had they not consulted Dr. Feldman who knew that Jane had a wild imagination and was not capable of hurting anyone. She glanced at her daughter on the video monitor and wondered what she was thinking.

Beth's comments had hurt Jane. She wanted to tell the court that Beth would have no way of knowing whether or not she had friends because Beth lived in Toxteth and had not seen her in months. I do have friends, thought Jane, as a tear rolled down her cheek. She felt that she had been accused of being crazy yet was not allowed to speak in her own defence. She desperately wanted to explain that she had not been serious when she talked of kidnapping Beth and stitching her face. She wanted to tell them about *The Nightmare Before Christmas*, and about Sally, the doll with the stitched face.

During a break in the proceedings, Helen phoned her sister. "It's not going well," she said shakily. "I don't think they are going to release Jane. Can you come to the courthouse as soon as possible? I might need you to act as surety."

"Seriously? What is wrong with those people?" responded Emily in disbelief. "Why don't they just give themselves a shake!"

Jack and Emily jumped into their car and raced to the courthouse. As Helen was explaining the gravity of the situation to them, Janet Hale appeared. She did not inspire confidence. Both Jack and Emily assumed that she was one of the cleaning staff. Helen made the introductions and Janet handed Emily a form to complete. Then they filed back into the courtroom.

Emily looked up at the video monitor and saw Jane wearing handcuffs and the little striped sweater that she had bought for her at American Eagle. This is a nightmare, she thought.

Natalie Coughlin insisted that Jane was dangerous and should not be released into the custody of her mother. It was as though Helen were a complete stranger and not to be trusted. Ms. Coughlin wanted Jane detained under Section 16 of the Mental Health Act. In order to comply with the wishes of the Crown, Janet Hale suggested that if Jane were released into her mother's custody, she would agree to immediately take her daughter to Southern Ontario Hospital for a mental health assessment. She sent Helen out of the courtroom to make an appointment at Southern Ontario Hospital. This, however, did not satisfy the Crown.

Janet then suggested that Jane's aunt and uncle had agreed to act as surety. Emily took the witness stand and was questioned by Natalie Coughlin.

"Please state your name and address."

"Emily Morrison. I am Jane Collins' aunt and I live in Toronto which is about an hour away from Toxteth."

"Does Jane have a driver's license?"

"Well, no. She is only fourteen-years-old. I have a bedroom with a lock on the door and I will watch Jane day and night. I will not let her out of my sight."

"What would you do if she were to disappear?"

"I would immediately notify the police."

Helen breathed a sigh of relief. Her sister had given the correct response. She did not know that this had been an exercise in futility, a cruel charade, since it had already been decided that Jane was not to be released under any circumstances. Unbeknownst to Helen or Janet Hale, the head Crown, Lynne Thomas, had decided that bail was to be denied.

Natalie Coughlin insisted that Jane be held under section 16 of the Mental Health Act and JP H. N. L. Woods ordered that she be taken into custody. Helen, Jack and Emily left the courtroom in shock.

Handcuffed and terrified, Jane was transported in a police cruiser to Southern Ontario Hospital for a mental health assessment as ordered by JP H. N. L. Woods. Jack left to pick up Stephen and Emily drove Helen to the hospital hoping to see Jane.

Two large, armed, male police officers escorted a handcuffed Jane into the emergency department of the hospital where her mother and aunt were waiting. People stared at the prisoner. Helen and Emily introduced themselves to the two young police officers who in turn gave their names as P. C. Mills and P. C. Stevens. When asked if the handcuffs could be removed to save Jane further embarrassment, the officers refused, saying that they had cuffed her in front instead of behind her back as a compromise, but could not remove the cuffs. However, Jane could. She easily slipped them off her small hands. The officers agreed that, since they did not have a child-size pair of handcuffs, they could remain off. The Section 16 order was given to the triage nurse and a long wait in the emergency department began.

Jane whispered to her mother that she needed to use the washroom. "I think I'm bleeding, Mom," she said in a panic. "I need to get a pad in the washroom." The police officers escorted Jane and her mother to the public washroom. "Leave the door open," ordered one of them.

Despite it being a public area and Helen going into the washroom with her daughter, the police refused to allow them to close the door. The officers stood at the open door as Helen tried to shield her daughter from the eyes of people walking past. Jane was mortified.

"They wouldn't dare do that to an adult," said Emily in disgust. "We should lodge a complaint against them."

"You can't complain about the police," said Helen. "They can do whatever they want and get away with it!"

If the police officers and the triage nurse had read the Section 16 order, they would have understood that the examination was to be conducted by a qualified physician. As a result of their incompetence, Jane was examined by Steve Cook, the Youth Crisis Counsellor who happened to be on call that day. No one thought to contact Dr. Feldman or any other qualified physician despite the fact that Mr. Cook wrote, in his report, that Jane was Dr. Feldman's patient.

"I don't want Jane to be alone with a Crisis Counsellor," whispered Helen to her sister.

"I think Jane has a legal right to have someone with her. It's her decision," answered Emily.

When Steve Cook finally called Jane into his office, Helen and Emily trooped in behind her. They explained to him that another Crisis Counsellor at the Hospital had unnecessarily given Jane's personal health information to the police, resulting in a charge being laid. Clearly irritated by their presence, Steve Cook regarded the two sisters with disdain.

"As professionals we have an obligation to report issues that may put a patient or others at risk," he said officiously. "Now, I need you both to leave my office."

"Would you like us to leave, Jane?" asked Emily. Jane nodded. She did not want her mother and aunt to hear what she was about to say.

At first Jane had been afraid to speak to Steve. She knew that bad things could happen as a result of speaking to hospital counsellors. However, she was desperate to unburden herself and tell someone about her frightening and disappointing weekend. She told Steve that her father had touched her inappropriately, offered her alcohol and cigarettes and had wanted to sleep with her. When asked if there had been any other times when someone had physically, emotionally, verbally or sexually abused her, Jane told him that a boy named Brad had raped her the previous Easter. Steve wrote down all of the details and later informed the Children's Aid Society of suspected child abuse. Jane then talked about her love of music, movies and writing stories. Steve concluded that she was not dangerous or homicidal. Relieved that she would not be admitted to Southern Ontario Hospital, Jane thought that she was free to go home with her mother. She wondered if Boston Pizza was still open.

When advised that Jane was not being admitted to Southern Ontario Hospital, the officers informed Helen that Jane would be taken to the Jarvis Street Detention Centre in Toronto. The fact remained that she had been charged with a crime and bail had been denied. An ashen-faced Jane was led away between the two police officers who towered over her. Emily put an arm around her weeping sister as they watched the police cruiser drive off into the night.

15.

Doing Hard Time

Most of the prisoners at the Jarvis Street Detention Centre had been charged with serious crimes, were male and older than Jane. The employees were mystified when she was handed over to them for processing. This involved a full body strip search. Many young men had cried when subjected to such harsh treatment. Jane was so humiliated, when ordered to remove all of her clothing, spread her legs and bend over, that she truly wanted to die. I am not Jane, she told herself. My name is Holly. After the strip search, she was given a large prison outfit to wear. The pants were so big that they reached her armpits.

Later that night, Helen received a phone call from a female employee of the Jarvis Street Detention Centre. The woman said that she did not understand why a young girl who had been charged with such a minor offense had been sent to them. "It must have been a mistake," she said. "I can assure you that your daughter will be transferred to a different facility tomorrow."

On Tuesday morning Helen awoke with a start. She felt sick with worry upon realizing that she had no idea where Jane had been taken. As she began phoning the detention centre in a frantic effort to locate her, the telephone beeped, indicating that a caller was on the other line. That must be them, she thought, as she eagerly took the call.

An officious woman from the Children's Aid Society was on the phone talking about a possible case of child abuse reported by Steve Cook of Southern Ontario Hospital. The woman insisted that she needed to speak to Jane Collins and her family.

"I'm sorry, she is unavailable," said Helen wishing that she had ignored the beeping phone. "Could you please call back later, I am very busy at the moment."

The woman warned that an investigation was imminent and the CAS would not be ignored.

Helen contacted the detention centre and was advised that Jane had been sent to a facility in the west end of Toronto. She then left several urgent phone messages for a lawyer, Cliff Goodman, and waited all day, but he did not respond. Angrily, she tried to call Tracey Hogan to ask why she had betrayed her daughter's confidence, but Ms. Hogan could not be reached. Helen was never able to speak with her again.

Earlier that morning Jane had been awakened by pounding on her cell wall at the detention centre. "Hey, who're you and what're you in for?" asked a deep male voice.

Each prisoner had a job to do before breakfast. Jane was ordered to scrub prison doors. Breakfast consisted of one cup of juice, one cup of milk and five slices of bread. A large youth, sitting next to Jane at the table, volunteered that he was being held in custody for aggravated assault. "Why you here little girl?" he asked.

After breakfast the prisoners were taken to a gym and encouraged to play basketball. Jane did not feel comfortable playing with the large male inmates and explained that she was unable to run because her shoelaces had been taken from her. She was later transported to a facility in the west end of the city.

On the fifth of September, instead of starting grade nine at St. Joan of Arc Catholic School, Jane spent the day in a detention centre watching TV and chatting with her new friends: André, Tyrone, Winston and Dwayne.

Emily and Helen were unfamiliar with the west end of Toronto but managed to find directions to the facility online through MapQuest. They had read stories of gang wars and murders in this area of the city. Surveying their surroundings, upon arrival at the centre, they were leery about leaving the safety of their car. A group of teenagers sitting on the stoop of a house across the street regarded the two women menacingly.

A worker opened the door of the facility and introduced himself as Lorne. He was a friendly young man who invited them inside and offered coffee while they waited for Jane to join them at a rickety table beside a small kitchen. Above the table, thumbtacked to a bulletin board, were posters warning of the evils of drug abuse. A dark sheet hung over the window blocking out the light and the dingy living room was lit by the glow of a TV being watched by four large young men and a small girl. They were watching a show called *Prison Break*.

"Hi Mom, hi Auntie Em," said Jane. She was wearing a large orange shirt that looked like a nightgown on her petite frame.

"How are you, sweetheart?" asked Helen as she hugged her daughter.

"I'm okay Mom, but I need to show you and Auntie Em something. I'll be right back." She ran up the stairs and returned with a little faded bundle. "They ruined my new sweater. I told them it wasn't dirty but they took it away from me and washed it anyway. They must have used boiling water because the colours have faded and it shrank. Now it's too tight," she said sadly.

"Oh, I'll buy you another one, Jane. They're on sale now," Emily assured her with a smile.

Helen gave her daughter a bag of potato chips and a chocolate bar.

"Thanks Mom. I'm going to share this with my friends later," she said.

Helen's cell phone rang as she and Emily sat with Jane. "Thank God," she whispered to her sister. "It's Cliff Goodman, the lawyer who was recommended to me. I've been leaving him messages for the past couple of days."

"Hello Mr. Goodman. Thanks for getting back to me. I didn't explain the circumstances in my voice message and I'm not sure that you are aware of the background information."

"Okay, well, my fourteen-year-old daughter, Jane, was charged with uttering a threat. We went to court yesterday and I couldn't find anyone to represent her because of the holiday so we had Janet Hale as Duty Counsel."

"Yes I know I should have had it put over but I didn't and Jane was denied bail."

"She is being held in custody."

"She's in jail! I'm sitting with her in a detention centre right now!"

"She will be back in court tomorrow and I would like to retain you to represent her. Please can you help us?"

"I want you to do whatever is necessary to have her released."

"I want you to get her out of here!"

"Tomorrow, September 6th."

"Okay. Thanks Cliff. Bye"

"Is he going to be my lawyer?" asked Jane.

"Yes, Mr. Goodman said that he will be there for you tomorrow."

Helen turned to her sister. "Cliff said that he is scheduled to be Duty Counsel in Youth Court tomorrow and he will meet us there."

"Are you sure he won't be too busy with other cases?" asked Emily.

"No, I've explained the situation to him. He knows how serious this is. It's so unusual. They almost never deny bail, especially to a young person."

"Mom," Jane called as Helen and Emily were about to leave, "can I get my hair done in cornrows like André?"

16.

September 6

On the sixth of September, Justice Kendall was sitting in his chambers contemplating the new Community Treatment Court that he had initiated. Eagerly he anticipated its commencement on September thirteenth. This special court would hear cases involving mentally ill persons accused of crimes, and instead of sentencing them to time in custody, they would be asked to seek counselling, sign peace bonds and the like. It made sense that people suffering from mental illnesses, and thus not responsible for their actions, should be dealt with differently. Justice Kendall became aware of Jane's case.

A serious young Child and Youth Worker named Cynthia escorted Jane to the courthouse from the detention centre. There, they were met by Helen, her son James, Emily and Jack, all of whom believed that Jane would be home that afternoon and starting grade nine the following day. Jane hugged them all and thanked them for coming.

"I can't wait to get home and see Sandy, Jynx and Felix," she said. "How are the pets doing James? Do they miss me?"

"They'll be happy to see you," said James giving his sister another hug.

James smiled at Cynthia. "It's crazy that my sister has spent two nights in jail," he said. Cynthia did not return his smile nor did she make any comment. James shrugged. Guess she's not the friendly type, he thought.

"This whole thing is ridiculous," said Emily.

"Let's hope that Cliff Goodman is able to put an end to it," said Jack.

"He has a pretty good reputation," Helen said hopefully.

Cliff Goodman was a handsome, charming, generous lawyer, well liked and well respected by all who had the pleasure of working with him at the Newton courthouse. Always the life of the party, he often played Santa Claus at Christmas gatherings and handed out candy and gifts. Everyone adored Cliff.

Helen was surprised when she learned that Jane's case had been moved from Youth Court to another courtroom and was to be heard by Justice Kendall. Once inside the courtroom she felt hopeful upon recognizing Crown attorney Paul Hedley whom she knew had children of his own. Surely he would understand that Jane was an innocent young person who did not belong in jail but rather in school. Cliff rushed over from Youth Court and sat next to Jane. He flashed a friendly reassuring smile at her and she drew a sigh of relief.

Justice Kendall angrily struck down the Section 16 order, since it had apparently been issued in error by the JP. Then he put the case over until September thirteenth. Cliff Goodman looked taken aback. He muttered a few words and then it was over.

"What just happened?" asked Emily.

"It's over," said Helen in disbelief. "Maybe Justice Kendall isn't aware that Jane is being held in custody. I just cannot believe that he really intended to send a fourteen-year-old girl back to jail for a week, but that's what he has done."

Outside the courtroom, the family approached Cliff Goodman.

"Please do something!" shouted Emily.

"Who are you?" asked Cliff.

"I'm Jane's aunt and I want you to get her out of this mess right now! She belongs in school, not jail! You're her lawyer. Do something!"

As Jack led Emily and James down the stairs to buy some coffee in the cafeteria, Cliff turned to Helen. "I'll speak to the Crown attorney," he said.

An hour later, he emerged from his meeting with Paul Hedley. "I'm sorry," he said. "There is nothing more I can do at this point. The case has been put over until September thirteenth and your daughter will be held in custody until then. I am so sorry." With that, he shook hands with Helen and Jane and gave them each his card.

"Mom," said a tearful Jane, "tomorrow is Thursday. Could you please call Mr. Reynolds and tell him I'm sick and can't come for my music lesson. Oh, did you call my school?"

"Yes sweetheart, I told Mr. Monardo that you were sick, and I'll call Mr. Reynolds as soon as I get home," answered Helen as she hugged her daughter tightly, never wanting to let her go. Cynthia grasped Jane firmly by the upper arm and marched her away from her mother. As she was forcefully led down the stairs toward the exit, for the drive back to jail, Jane's plaintive sobs echoed through the courthouse.

17.

Cool Friends

Jane's new friends had not expected to see her again and were intrigued when she returned to the facility that afternoon.

"S'up my wigger? C'mon girl, what did you really do?" asked Winston.

"I robbed a convenience store at gunpoint," replied Jane with her chin in the air, hoping that no one would notice she had been crying. "I'll be getting out of here soon though. I have a good lawyer." She proudly showed Winston the card that Cliff Goodman had given her.

Winston sucked his teeth loudly. "Most of the brothers are in here for breach," he said. "Your lawyer ain't worth shit."

Jane wondered if he was right.

At "quiet time" the prisoners were sent to their rooms to read, sleep or meditate in silence. This usually had a calming effect and gave the staff a break. Jane requested some paper and a pen or pencil in order to do some writing, but was told that sharp objects were forbidden. The substitutes, a box of crayons and a colouring book, evoked warm memories of happy times spent colouring with her grandmother when she was very young. When Grandma had died unexpectedly, just after Jane's fifth birthday, she had discarded her crayons. Helen found them in the garbage bin along with a colouring book.

Since there was no one around to pass judgment, Jane selected an orange crayon from the box of Crayolas and began bringing Donald Duck's large beak to life. Then, as she coloured his sailor jacket and hat a deep navy blue, she was reminded of her grandfather. Not only was Grandpa able to draw a good likeness of Donald Duck, but he also had the same funny, explosive temper as the cartoon character. Sitting alone in the dismal little room, Jane longed for her grandparents and wondered what they would think if they were alive and could see what had befallen their granddaughter. *I guess they would wish they were dead,* she thought as she coloured the sky a pale shade of blue.

Later in the day, as Jane and her friends watched wrestling on the small TV, Dwayne turned to her and asked, "Can I put my hand in your shirt?"

"Okay," replied Jane," not wanting to make any enemies. She felt very intimidated by the young men and was afraid of what might happen if they were to turn against her. A few moments later, André, without saying a word, thrust his hand down the front of her jeans. Jane looked around for a worker, but there was no one to help her.

The two sisters wandered around the grocery store searching for healthy treats to give Jane and her friends. They were beginning to feel a little more comfortable in the neighbourhood and were not quite so nervous.

"How about this?" suggested Emily, picking up a bag of Smartsnack in the health food section. "It's low fat, low sodium and has no hydrogenated oil."

Helen shook her head. "Somehow, I don't think the guys would thank you for that."

"I guess you're right," said Emily as she grabbed five bags of potato chips and placed them on the counter.

The young men seemed surprised but thanked Emily as she handed each of them a bag of chips, all but André, who rarely smiled and had not uttered a word to anyone since coming to the detention centre. He sat sullenly on the couch watching TV. Emily wondered what his story was as she handed him the chips.

"Lucky Tyrone got to leave today. His mama came and picked him up," said Jane. "I guess he's at home now and can go to school tomorrow. He's in grade twelve."

"But I gave out five bags of chips," said Emily."

"That guy over there just came here today. He's in for armed robbery," whispered Jane, pointing to a young man sitting in the shadows. "His name is Eddie but his street name is Byron. My street name is Holly," she added. "Why am I still in jail when Tyrone got to leave? When can I get out of here?"

"Well, I think Mr. Goodman is too busy to help us," said Helen as she gently smoothed her daughter's hair back from her face. "He never returns my calls. So, I have retained another lawyer for you. His name is Mike Rivers and he's working hard to get you out of here as soon as possible."

Jane sucked her teeth. "Mr. Goodman ain't worth shit," she said.

"Jane Collins, don't use that kind of language," scolded Helen in surprise.

"Well, what do you expect," said her sister. "Look where she is."

As the two women left, Jane called out, "Bye, Mama. Later, Auntie Em."

Helen turned to her sister. "Mama?" she shrugged.

18.

Changes

Helen decided that Jane could no longer attend St. Joan of Arc Catholic School after what had happened. It was her feeling that the court would probably not allow it anyway since Beth Henderson was a student there. Besides, she thought, the police gave the Henderson family Jane's private information and Beth was certainly not trustworthy.

Accompanied by her son, James, she went to the Catholic School to advise of her daughter's transfer to the public system. There, they were met by a subdued Mr. Monardo. "Hello, Joe," he said, shaking James' hand. "Nice to see you Mrs. Collins, I am so sorry that little Jane has been ill."

"Well yes, she is still sick," said Helen. "But I'm here because Jane and I have decided that it would be a good idea for her to transfer to Allerton High School. It's only a five minute walk from our house and, frankly, she never felt safe from bullying in this school."

Mr. Monardo did not comment on the fact that he and his staff had failed in their obligation to ensure that students felt safe at school and were protected from bullying. "I completely understand," he said complacently.

"Well that's it," muttered Helen to her son, as they left the school, "the end of an important family tradition. Jane will be the only one in our entire family not to receive a Catholic education. She will never wear her Confirmation dress. Your grandmother would be devastated."

James put an arm around his mother as they walked away from the school, and Catholicism.

Helen's son Chris had begun a Computer Programming course at Seneca College and was now living with Emily, Jack, Stephen, Mark and Joe, who was still attending University. Everyone was concerned about Jane, and the boys were having difficulty concentrating on their studies. Each day they would ask if she had been released, only to be told that she was still in custody. Joe felt angry and bitter toward the police for failing to conduct a proper investigation. Chris was bewildered that anyone would seriously believe his little sister was dangerous. He knew that she was not capable of hurting anyone. James, who still lived at home, worried about his mother's declining health. She no longer ate properly or used her treadmill. He knew that she was on blood pressure medication and he often heard her crying at night. Mark was concerned that his cousin would be a changed person after such a horrible experience. Stephen typed on his alphabet board, "THIS IS AN UTTER TRAVESTY OF JUSTICE." Jack was extremely disappointed in the hospital, the police and the justice system. They had all failed his niece.

Every day after finishing work in the Newton courthouse, Helen met Emily at her home in Toronto and the two sisters drove to the detention centre to visit Jane. Jack stayed at the house to make dinner for the boys and to care for Stephen. On Friday, as they drove along the highway, Emily mentioned to her sister that she had called Southern Ontario Hospital and a Toronto based legal aid clinic called *Justice for Children and Youth*.

"You're not going to believe this, Helen," she began. "I phoned Southern Ontario Hospital and asked for Tracey Hogan's professional designation so you could lodge a complaint against her. I expected to find that she was a psychologist or a social worker. Well, she's a criminologist! The Director of Mental Health told me that she has a degree in criminology of all things!"

"My God!" said Helen. "That's probably why she never probed to find out where Jane's ideas had come from. She just interrogated her as if she were conducting a police investigation. And she never offered Jane any coping strategies. The only help she ever gave her was a kid's book called *What to Do When You're Scared & Worried*. Well, I guess if you're scared and worried, you don't talk to a hospital counsellor or you could end up being more scared and worried behind bars! Why would the hospital hire a criminologist to counsel troubled kids?"

"Good question! Oh yes, I nearly forgot, Hogan also has a Child and Youth Worker Certificate. That's what Stephen's workers have. You know, they sit with him in school and help him to communicate using supported typing. The staff hired to work in group homes also have those certificates. I don't think they are qualified to work in mental health facilities."

"It's entirely my fault. I should have asked for her qualifications before allowing her to speak to Jane."

"No, it's not your fault Helen! You took her there in good faith, expecting that the hospital would have hired competent staff to counsel young people."

"Even so, I should have thought to ask."

"I left my phone number with *Justice for Children and Youth*, continued Emily. "A very helpful lawyer returned my call. She told me that there is always a presumption in favour of bail for children and youth."

"Well, the reason why they didn't release Jane was because they thought she was crazy!"

"Yes, well the lawyer also told me that the courts are not to use detention in place of mental health services."

"But Steve Cook said she had no mental health issues and released her to the cops so they could drag her off to be strip searched and thrown in jail. That JP should never have denied bail."

"We should have had the presence of mind to insist that she be admitted to the hospital. I guess we were too shocked to think clearly."

"So many mistakes have been made."

Helen and Emily noticed changes in Jane at each visit. She was becoming increasingly anxious and despondent and had lost her innocence. At times she seemed like a stranger to them, but then the familiar Jane would return.

"Dwayne said that when he was strip searched they lifted up his penis to check for drugs," she informed her mother and aunt. "Sometimes the guys call him "G," that's short for gangster. I can't wait to get out of here Mama, I miss everyone and I'm really getting behind in my schoolwork. They try to teach us stuff here, but it's not the same."

"I have been meaning to talk to you about school, sweetheart. I think it would be good for you to make a fresh start and go to Allerton High for grade nine instead of Joan of Arc with all of those bullies. You could walk to school instead of being bussed."

"That would be cool Mom! I wouldn't have to wear that ugly uniform anymore. I could wear my regular clothes and nobody would spit on me or laugh at me. I wouldn't have to worry about being beaten up."

"I shouldn't have listened to Tracey when she told me that it would be a mistake for you to change schools. I should have followed my own instincts about getting you away from the bullies. I think it's more important for you to feel safe than it is to get a Catholic education. I know that giving up your Confirmation is disappointing but God will understand."

"Fuck religion!" Jane shouted for all to hear.

"Oh my God," said Emily. "We have to get her out of here! What kind of fucked up legal system would put a little girl in this terrible environment. Oops, sorry. Never use bad language like that Jane. It makes you sound ignorant."

As they drove home in silence, Helen stared into space despondently and Emily feared the worst.

19

Fourteen

On a warm Saturday evening, Emily was seated at a table in Fran's Restaurant, dreamily gazing through the window at the sooty Victorian bricks of Massey Hall across the street. She imagined that the grand old lady had probably not changed much since she first opened her doors in 1894. A small line of people that had begun to form at her entrance was now snaking its way along the sidewalk and around the street corner. The Fab Faux, a Beatles tribute band, was scheduled to perform.

"I love coming downtown," Helen was saying. "I miss living and working in Toronto. Allerton has never really felt like home."

"We should order our food now," said Jack. "The concert starts at eight."

Emily smiled. "What a great menu," she said. "It's so retro, just like the décor. I think I'll have the meatloaf and a piece of apple pie with cheese for dessert. I wonder if they have Cherry Coke."

"I'm just having a tuna sandwich and a coffee," said Helen.

The waitress appeared and Jack ordered for the three of them.

As he sipped his beer, Jack imagined his young niece having her evening meal among criminals. He felt sick with worry but hoped that Helen and Emily were able to put Jane's situation out of their minds for the evening and enjoy a brief reprieve.

Helen had no appetite and was tormented by feelings of guilt for being free to walk the streets of Toronto while her daughter's freedom had been denied. She reproached herself for taking Jane to Southern Ontario Hospital. It's entirely my fault, she thought miserably. Although she agonized over the fate of her child, she made an effort to appear happy for the sake of Jack and Emily who had purchased the concert tickets.

Emily was able to control her anger and feign lightheartedness for the sake of her sister and husband.

The Fab Faux gave an inspired performance and the middle-aged crowd sang and clapped appreciatively. To Helen's eye, the atmosphere was surreal. As she watched happy gray-haired adults dancing in the aisles, she imagined her fourteen-year-old daughter languishing in a miserable, frightening detention centre.

As the band sang, Emily closed her eyes and was momentarily transported back in time to a Beatles concert long ago at Maple Leaf Gardens. She and her friends, Ellen, Joan and Dora had screamed and cried during the entire performance. They had been deliriously happy. Emily recalled taking the day off school and standing in the rain for hours to purchase the Beatles tickets. She had been thrilled to meet Bob McAdorey from CHUM radio station as he handed out CHUM charts to the soaking wet fans. She recalled ironing her hair with her mother's steam iron and wearing a blue "poor boy" sweater with white jeans to the concert. Ellen and Dora had stood on their seats waving a handmade sign that read "We love you Ringo." Joan held up a "Love you George" sign and Emily simply danced up and down on her seat screaming "John" throughout the concert. How wonderful to have been an innocent, carefree fourteen-year-old.

Emily tried to imagine her fourteen-year-old self being bullied at school, betrayed by a trusted adult, then arrested and led away in handcuffs to be strip searched and put in jail among older male criminals. She did not believe that she could have survived such an ordeal. Her heart ached for Jane. Fourteen was such a vulnerable age.

Helen, Jack and Emily joined the audience in giving The Fab Faux several standing ovations. Then, as they walked out into the night air, they agreed that it had been a lovely evening.

20.

September 13

On the thirteenth of September Jane was brought to the Newton courthouse by Lorne, her favourite worker. He was a friendly young man who shook hands with Helen, Emily and Jack. They were impressed that he had stopped in the cafeteria to buy a Cookies 'n Cream bar for Jane, her favourite. As they waited outside the courtroom, Cliff Goodman approached Jane and sat next to her with a friendly grin.

"He must still think he's Jane's lawyer," whispered Helen to Emily and Jack. "I guess he didn't listen to my voice message. I told him that since he seemed too busy to take the case, I had retained someone else."

Jane told Cliff that she was waiting for Mike Rivers. He patted her head and left.

Unlike Cliff Goodman, Mike was not a warm, charming sort of man. Rather, he was ill-tempered, aggressive and brusque. Practicing law for many years had made him exceedingly cynical about the Canadian judicial system. Jane was afraid of him at first. Helen, Emily and Jack liked his style. He was against the idea of Jane's case being heard in Justice Kendall's Community Treatment Court. He knew that there was a stigma attached to having one's case heard in a special court for accused persons with mental health problems. Helen had advised him that Jane would refuse to sign a Peace Bond or speak to a counsellor. Therefore the CTC court was simply out of the question.

The court appearance was short. The case was put over until the eighteenth of September and Jane was to remain in custody for at least five more days. Helen was devastated and appeared bewildered and close to tears. Jane wept as Lorne led her away from her mother, again.

Mike explained to Helen, Emily and Jack, that it would be necessary for him to obtain the Disclosure before making an application for a bail review. This process, he said, normally took several business days to complete.

"I don't believe this!" cried Emily. "Jane did nothing wrong! All she did was talk to an incompetent counsellor!"

"You weren't there!" Mike snapped back fiercely.

"Don't you raise your voice to me, mister!" shouted Emily in anger and frustration.

"Get away from me," said Mike through clenched teeth.

Jack led Emily toward the cafeteria and away from Mike. As they sat drinking coffee, JP Woods, dressed in her black robes, drifted past the door. Suddenly enraged, Emily lost control of herself, and before Jack had a chance to stop her, raced out of the cafeteria and tore up the stairs after the JP.

"You sent my fourteen-year-old niece to jail!" she shouted as Woods looked away. "She's still there!" she continued as the JP motioned to two police officers. Emily quickly bolted back down the stairs and into the cafeteria. As she sat with Jack sipping her coffee, the police approached their table. The female Officer smiled.

"There isn't going to be a problem here is there?" she asked.

"No Officer," replied Emily smiling sweetly.

Jack and Emily remained at the table, waiting for Helen, oblivious to the humming of the air conditioner until, all at once, it fell silent and the cafeteria was in darkness. The sudden power failure meant evacuation of the building and everyone filed through the courthouse doors and into the humid air outside. Black clouds gathered in the sky above and a heavy rain began to fall. As they sheltered in the entranceway among judges, lawyers and hapless accused persons, Jack and Emily searched the crowd for Helen, but she was nowhere to be seen. Then, in the distance, they spotted a lone figure, soaking wet and walking slowly through the teeming rain toward her car. This image of her sister would haunt Emily for years to come.

As Jane walked back into the detention centre clutching a small teddy bear that Lorne had bought for her, the young inmates made no comment. Although curious as to why she was among them yet again, they understood her disappointment and left her alone.

Lorne searched the closet and found a baseball. "Would anyone like to throw this around outside," he asked. Jane and Winston jumped at the chance. As Lorne gently threw the ball to her, Jane wished that he were her dad. Mom should have married someone like him, she thought, instead of that other guy.

When they went back inside, Jane, Winston and the others were advised that they would all be transferred to alternative detention centres since the current location would be closing temporarily. It was to become a facility for girls only. Jane wondered if the staff somehow knew that two of the boys had touched her. Although she had not been happy there, she was afraid of being sent to another facility and wanted to remain with the inmates and staff that she had come to know.

Jack found directions to the new detention centre on MapQuest and printed them while Helen phoned to ask about visiting hours. She was surprised and disappointed when told that visitors were only allowed twice weekly. Jane had become accustomed to seeing her mother and aunt every day and Helen worried that her daughter might be upset and frightened at the new facility. She desperately wanted to see her daughter but the rules were strictly enforced.

"This is not a holiday camp," said an unpleasant woman at the other end of the phone. "You can visit tomorrow."

As they drove along the Don Valley Parkway on their way to the detention centre, Helen turned to her sister and grinned. "I heard a funny story at the courthouse today," she said. "Norma was in the washroom last Wednesday afternoon when she heard someone crying like a child in one of the stalls. It was JP Woods. She told Norma that she had been accosted in the hallway. Apparently, a woman chased her up the stairs and shouted at her."

Emily parked her car beside a large house in an unfamiliar area of Scarborough. As she and Helen walked up the pathway toward the door, they heard a voice call from a second floor window. Looking up, they saw a young girl. "Are y'all here to see Holly?" she shouted.

"No," replied Emily.

"Maybe she means Jane," suggested Helen as she rang the doorbell. "She probably doesn't want anyone here to know her name."

An unkempt little woman wearing a scowl on her pasty face opened the door. "We're here to visit Jane Collins," said Helen. "I'm Helen Collins, her mother, and this is my sister Emily.

The woman did not introduce herself. "We don't allow aunts," she said, glancing at Emily. "You'll have to wait outside."

"You see, I'm a single mother and I don't have anyone else for support. Since Jane doesn't have a father to visit her, can her aunt be substituted, please?" pleaded Helen.

"Well, okay, just this once," sighed the woman.

This detention centre was very different from the previous one. It was dirty and unpleasant, the workers were unfriendly and most of the prisoners were female. Two scruffy young teens wearing sweat-suits, sat at a small table playing cards. A pretty girl wearing pink pyjamas came dancing into the room singing a song called "SOS." Helen and Emily recognized her as the girl who had called to them from the window.

"My auntie will be coming to see me," she told a staff member.

"She won't be allowed to see you Latoya," sneered the worker.

Then Jane came running into the room and threw her arms around Helen. She looked alarmingly pale and her eyes were red from crying. "Please, I can't stay here!" she gasped. "The people here are so mean. They call me and the other girls losers and tell us that we will never amount to anything. My room is so dirty that it makes me feel sick to be in it. Honestly Mom, the mattress is all stained, the sheets are dirty and the pillow is yellow and crusty. There are boogers all over the walls. It's disgusting! Please! I'll die if I have to stay here! I want you and Auntie Em to come and see the disgusting room they put me in."

"This is the visiting area. You are not allowed to take anyone to your room," snapped the worker.

Jane burst into tears. "Don't leave me here Mom!" she cried. "I'll kill myself if I have to stay here!" She began to sweat profusely and hyperventilate. Her heart pounded rapidly.

"Oh God, she's having a panic attack," moaned Helen.

Jane sat on her mother's knee and Helen rocked her as they both cried. Emily wished that everyone responsible for putting her niece in such a foul place could witness this scene.

21.

September 18

Mike Rivers had worked diligently and succeeded in obtaining the Disclosure and a bail review on a timely basis. He was concerned that his young client had been in custody for two weeks. On Monday, the eighteenth of September, he made an effort to smile at Jane and Helen when he met them outside the courtroom. Clearly they were both terrified. Jane had been escorted to the courthouse by a friendly young man named Linton who said that he was mystified as to why she had been in custody for so long. He sat next to her, reading a paperback novel. Mark, who had taken the day off school to support his cousin, calmly chatted with her about movies and music videos. Mike eyed Emily with trepidation knowing that she had a volatile temperament, somewhat like his own. He shook her hand and Jack's, then cautioned the family not to speak in the courtroom.

When Helen saw that Justice Bloom was presiding, she felt heartened, believing him to be a reasonable man. Inside the courtroom, Jane sat with Mike, trying to keep her breathing under control. She feared having a panic attack as she watched him talking with the Crown attorney. His face became red as he wheeled his chair around to the family and cautioned them again not to make any comments regardless of what they might hear. Oh God, thought Helen, that means it's going to be brutal. Please put an end to this nightmare today, thought Emily as Jack squeezed her hand. Mark felt very frightened for his cousin as he watched her sitting next to her lawyer. She looked small and composed. I would probably freak out if that were me up there, he thought.

The Crown attorney, a young woman named Pam Hunter, stood up and advised the Judge that the Head Crown, Paul Hedley, had requested that the matter be put over for a few more days in order to obtain an outside Crown and judge. This would be necessary for the purpose of impartiality since the accused person's mother, Helen Collins, was a court employee.

It seemed to Helen that the room had become airless. She had difficulty breathing as she struggled to compose herself. This was incomprehensible. Paul Hedley wanted to send Jane back to jail for a few more days because her mother worked at the courthouse! His children had been in school for the first two weeks of September while her daughter had been languishing in jail. She was certain that he had known from the start that she was a court employee.

Mike Rivers pleaded with Justice Bloom to hear the case. He appealed to the judge's sense of decency and compassion.

Justice Bloom looked at Jane, then made eye contact with Jack and nodded his head. He acknowledged that the accused was a young person who had missed the first two weeks of school. He claimed not to know Helen Collins and agreed to hear the case. There was an audible sigh of relief in the courtroom. Emily had a strong desire to utter a threat to Paul Hedley.

Pam Hunter read the allegations against Jane to the Court. Mark recognized the *Nightmare Before Christmas* scenario and rolled his eyes. Idiots, he thought. Why wouldn't they let Jane explain? Why didn't the police just ask her why she had said those things and she could have told them it was just a movie plot?

The Crown was not satisfied just to read the allegations. A recording had been made of Tracey Hogan's interview with the police, and Ms. Hunter insisted that it would be necessary to play it in open court for all to hear. Justice Bloom allowed it.

As Jane listened to her private thoughts being paraphrased and misconstrued by Tracey to the police, she felt as though she were sitting in the courtroom completely naked. She was absolutely mortified. Why are they doing this to me, she wondered. I just wanted help to make the bullying stop. I will never trust anyone again. It's not fair that they won't let me explain my side of it, she thought. She knew that many of the things that Tracey was saying in the recorded interview were untrue, as did her mother. Tracey had twisted everything but they were not allowed to refute what was being accepted as the undeniable truth. Jane turned and looked at her mother who was powerless to help. She could only sit and observe her hapless daughter's complete humiliation at the hands of the hospital, the police and the justice system.

It was excruciating for Jane's family members to listen to her private conversations with Tracey being played in open court. Mike Rivers, Linton, the Court Reporter, Marianne and Norma, the Clerk also found it harrowing to hear the recording and to witness Jane's embarrassment. Even Justice Bloom appeared uncomfortable as he observed the small girl before him, who hung her head.

Helen was surprised to hear Tracey say that she had encouraged Mrs. Collins to press charges against Nadia but that she did not believe her advice had been followed. Helen distinctly remembered that Tracey had requested the copies of the MSN bullying in order that she herself might fax them to a friend in the police department.

After listening to the recording, court was recessed for lunch. Jane relished the simple pleasure of walking across the street with Linton and her family to have a bite to eat at McDonald's. "Do you think the judge will let me go home today, Uncle Jack?" she whispered as he paid for her chicken nuggets.

"Yes I do Jane," he said with a hug. Helen and Emily were not so sure. After lunch Jack kissed them goodbye and went home to meet Stephen after his day program.

When court resumed, Justice Bloom indicated that he might "fashion a form of release." It was therefore necessary for Helen, as surety, to take the witness stand. Mike Rivers asked the usual questions one would ask at a bail hearing. Helen agreed to ensure that Jane attend school and have no contact with Beth Henderson. She advised the court that her daughter was registered at Allerton High, the local school and would no longer be attending St. Joan of Arc Catholic School in the town of Toxteth, where Beth Henderson was a student. Mike's questions had been brief and logical.

Pam Hunter asked numerous questions that seemed obscure and absurd. Helen felt nervous and resentful but made an effort to compose herself and answer politely. The names "Trevor" and "Monica" were presented as possible victims that Jane had mentioned to Tracey Hogan. Helen explained that her daughter knew two boys named Trevor. Trevor Allen was a student at St. Joan of Arc School and Trevor Brown was a friend who lived in Toronto. She stated that she did not believe that Jane had plans to harm either of these boys, nor a girl named Monica. It was all nonsense.

Ms. Hunter then asked about a boy named Matt. Helen explained that he had been a friend of Beth who had apparently expressed an interest in Jane. It was her understanding that Beth had initiated the bullying due to normal teenage jealously. These explanations did not satisfy the Crown who seemed to believe that there was something more sinister involved. She mentioned to Helen that her daughter had spent five days in a psychiatric unit at Toronto Hospital.

"No," said Helen. "It was only a weekend. She was admitted on a Friday night and then released early the following Monday morning."

Ms. Hunter referred to her notes. "No, you're wrong," she said emphatically. "Tracey Hogan said it was at least five days."

The Crown did not feel that Jane should be released unless strict bail conditions were imposed. She asked Helen to list the names and ages of those who resided with her in Allerton. Helen provided the names and ages of her three sons. Although Joe and Chris resided with Emily and Jack during the week while at University, they usually went home to Allerton on weekends and Helen believed the court would be more likely to release her daughter if it appeared there would be four adults to provide supervision in the home.

Ms. Hunter suggested to Justice Bloom that perhaps Jane should undergo an assessment at the Centre for Addiction and Mental Health (CAMH) in Toronto. He agreed that this was a good idea and was handed a form to complete. Apparently, without giving a thought to the hardship he was imposing on Jane and her mother, Justice Bloom went down the list of possible tests provided by CAMH and ticked every single box. This would mean that Jane would be subjected to three days of testing at the centre in Toronto and Helen would be required to take three days away from work, without pay, to drive her daughter to the appointments. Mike Rivers felt that it was intrusive, unnecessary, unjust and punitive for his young client to be subjected to a mental health assessment. She had, after all, been assessed by Dr. Feldman at Southern Ontario Hospital. He asked for permission to speak to his client and her mother outside the courtroom.

"I'll do anything if they will just let me go home," Jane said to Mike in the small meeting room.

"You don't have to agree to everything," he told Jane and her mother.

"Jane is afraid to speak to anyone after what happened with Tracey, but I think she understands now that she should just smile and say very little to these people. I think she can do it Mike. If it means getting bail, she will do it," said Helen.

"Is there any reason why you would need to be in Toxteth?" Mike asked.

"Well, the Dairy Queen is there," said Jane. "But I guess I could just eat regular ice cream for a while. And I won't be going to the Catholic school anymore, so, no. I don't need to go to Toxteth."

Back in the courtroom, Justice Bloom granted bail to Jane on the understanding that she had agreed to undergo a thorough Mental Health assessment at CAMH. He read aloud the following bail conditions:

1.   Reside with surety (mother).
2.   Abstain from communicating, directly or indirectly, with Beth Henderson or Trevor Allen.
3.   Not attend at or within 500 metres of the known place of residence, employment, or education of Beth Henderson or Trevor Allen.
4.   Observe a curfew to be in her residence at all times except in the presence of surety (mother) or brothers Joseph Collins or James Collins, or except while at school.
5.   Abstain from the consumption or possession of alcoholic beverages and non-medically prescribed drugs or narcotics.
6.   Continue such assessment and such counselling with Dr. Feldman (or his designate) and not stop that counselling without the permission of your surety (mother).
7.   Attend school at Allerton High School, Allerton ON.
8.   Not attend in the former "Town" of Toxteth ON or at St. Joan of Arc High School in Toxteth Ontario.
9.   Not to communicate directly or indirectly with Trevor Brown except with his written revocable consent to be filed with surety (mother: Helen Collins).

As Justice Bloom read the weapons prohibition imposed on Jane, he rolled his eyes: "Does not possess any firearm, crossbow, prohibited weapon, restricted weapon, prohibited device, ammunition, prohibited ammunition or explosive substance as defined by the Criminal Code of Canada.

Does not possess or apply for any authorization, license or registration certificate relating to the above-named items.

Surrenders all above-named items and every authorized, license and registration certificate related thereto in her possession as follows: None declared, but assuming it would otherwise apply, s. 115 of the Criminal Code shall not apply to this order.

TAKE NOTICE that a copy of the release document entered into as a result of this order shall be sent to the Chief Firearms Officer."

With that, everyone left the courtroom. Helen, Jane, Emily and Mark proceeded to the Surety Release room, and Linton, whose services were no longer required, said goodbye. When Helen briefly reentered the courtroom to retrieve her coat, she saw Justice Bloom who mentioned to her that he understood the bail conditions were harsh. He promised to relax them in a short while.

After the bail conditions had been typed, they were read to Helen and Jane inside the Surety Release room. Helen signed as the surety and Jane shakily wrote her name above the line that said "Signature of Accused." This means that I am different from other people, she thought. I am no good.

22.

House Arrest

Emily chuckled as they left the courthouse. "What lunacy," she said. "Forbidding Jane to own a crossbow, firearms or explosives is absurd."

Helen was not amused. "I have to work with those people who put my daughter in jail," she said angrily. "I have to look at them every day. They are my co-workers. They know me and they know what they have done to me and to Jane. And they don't care. It's just a cruel game to them. I wish I never had to set foot inside this courthouse again, but unfortunately I need to earn a living. Coming here every day is torture."

The foursome went to the Newton Mall to buy school clothes for Jane. Both women felt extremely nervous and ensured that Jane was never more than a few feet away from Helen. They were beginning to realize just what the restrictive bail conditions meant.

As Helen and Emily sat in the food court sipping coffee and their children ate ice cream, Jane's eyes suddenly widened. "Oh, no," she cried. "Mom, I forgot that Reynolds is in Toxteth! I won't be able to go for my music lessons!"

"I think it's cruel and ridiculous to bar a child from entering into an entire town," said Emily. "Jane is being treated like a pariah. It's like a John Wayne movie – "This town ain't big enough for both of us, pilgrim," – I have never heard of such a thing." she sighed.

Jane began to list the important things that were in the town of Toxteth: Reynolds Music, the Dairy Queen, McDonald's, the movie theatre, the Catholic School and her parish church. "I won't be able to study and make my Confirmation. Grandma would be so disappointed if she knew. I won't be able to take my music lessons, go to the movie theatre, McDonald's or to the Dairy Queen. I won't even be able to go to St. Joan of Arc Church. Maybe I'm the only person in the entire world who isn't allowed in the town of Toxteth. I'm an outlaw like Auntie Em said."

"It won't be for long Jane. Justice Bloom promised me that he would relax the bail conditions in a little while," said Helen.

When Jane walked through the door of her home in Allerton, Sandy barked excitedly and ran around the living room doing joyful figure eights. Jynx and Felix purred and rubbed themselves around her ankles. Jane rushed into her bedroom and sat on her bed cuddling Sandy in her arms. Her family stood in the doorway, relieved that she was home.

As she hugged her dog, Jane declared, *"I tried to get back for the longest time. All I kept saying to everybody was, "I want to go home" and they finally sent me home. Anyway Sandy, I'm home and this is my room, and I'm never going to leave Allerton again. And oh, Auntie Em, there really is no place like home!"*

Everyone breathed a sigh of relief. It seemed that the nightmare was over and Jane had returned unscathed. Helen cautioned her that the bail conditions meant she would only be allowed outside of the house unaccompanied for the purpose of attending school. "The police may be keeping an eye on you and if you are found outside without me, James or Joe, you could be arrested and taken back into custody," she warned.

"I guess that means I won't be able to make any friends at the new school. Kids will think I'm weird if I can't hang out after school."

"That can't be helped. You could invite your friends to the house after school."

"Mom," said Jane sadly, "I'm afraid to start the new school. I've missed three weeks because Allerton High started a week earlier than other schools. I'm nervous because I won't know anyone and what if the police have told the principal that I'm a jailbird?"

"That's confidential information Jane."

"Sure Mom, I've heard that before. That's what you said when I went to Southern Ontario Hospital for help. You told me that everything I said to Tracey would be confidential. I'll bet the police have told everyone at the school."

Helen knew that the grade nine students of Allerton High School had gone on a three day camping trip to help them make new friends. Most high schools did this, and important friendships were forged on these trips. Often at high school graduation ceremonies, valedictorians and graduating students would reminisce about the wonderful weekend spent getting acquainted at the beginning of grade nine. Helen was angry that Jane had been denied this opportunity. So many things had been taken from her. She had suffered so many losses and indignities. Helen reproached herself regularly for taking her daughter to Southern Ontario Hospital for help.

James and Joe were busy, active, young adults, seldom available to help their mother. James had a large circle of friends and a steady girlfriend. Helen rarely saw him. Joe, who lived in Toronto during the week, had a part-time job in Newton and spent most of his free time in Toxteth with his girlfriend, Kate. Helen knew that neither of the two would be available to escort their sister to any activities. That job would be hers. Without her mother, Jane would be confined to the house after school and on weekends and holidays. Helen felt trapped. She realized just how much her daughter would depend on her, and understood, only too well, how difficult it would be to spend so much time with a fourteen-year-old.

Jane was reminded of her first day of kindergarten as she and her mother walked to Allerton High School on Tuesday morning. Not only was she accompanied by her mother and wearing a new dress, as she had when she was five, but she also felt as nervous and apprehensive as she had on that momentous day long ago.

Mr. Moore, the Vice-Principal of Allerton High, greeted Helen and Jane warmly and Jane introduced herself as Holly Collins. Helen explained that "Holly" was a nickname, but from that day forward, the staff and students knew Jane as Holly. It was necessary for the grade nine students to choose two elective subjects but since Jane was so late in starting school, the courses that interested her had been filled. Mr. Walters, the guidance counsellor, did his best to find appropriate placements for her, but Jane was upset and apprehensive when told that she would be in the drama and grade ten photography classes. She was given her course calendar and directions to the first class. Suddenly she panicked. "No, not today," she said. "I'll start tomorrow."

"Don't be silly Jane. You need to start today. You have a lot of catching up to do," said Helen.

"No I said! I'm not going to class today!" Jane shouted.

It was so unlike her to behave in such a manner. Helen feared that Mr. Moore would think her odd for making such a scene, but he seemed to be an understanding man. "I'm sorry, my daughter is a very nervous girl and lately has been having panic attacks," Helen explained.

Mr. Moore and Mr. Walters were so kind to Jane that she relented and agreed to stay. Helen walked her daughter around the school to help familiarize her with the locations of her classes, then gave her a hug and went home.

Although she had intended to spend the day typing a transcript, Helen was so nervous that she continually peered out the window, expecting to see Jane come walking up the driveway at any moment. When she eventually returned home at the end of the day, Helen was anxious to hear all about school.

"Well, at lunchtime a group of girls said they were going to "punk" me. Then they grabbed my purse and took my lunch money," sighed Jane.

"Oh no, not more bullying," said Helen in dismay.

"But I had a good day Mom. I met a really nice boy in my photography class. His name is Daniel and he's eighteen."

"That seems strange, having a fourteen-year-old and an eighteen-year-old in the same class."

"The photography class is for everyone Mom. Daniel is in grade twelve. He's really nice and friendly. Girls are so mean."

"Not all girls are mean. You just need to give them a chance. It would be a good idea for you to try and make some girlfriends. You could have sleepovers and watch movies, make fudge and do girl stuff."

"Daniel and I want to go out and take some pictures for our photography class. I guess you'll have to come with us. That really sucks. He's going to think I'm weird, having my mom following me around."

Helen sighed. She was concerned about the four year age difference between Jane and Daniel but did not want her daughter to be lonely. Oh well, she thought, at least they'll have a chaperone.

When she arrived home from work on Wednesday, Jane introduced her to Daniel, his girlfriend, Rhiannon and a boy named Brendan. They looked alike. All three had black hair and nails, various facial piercings and black clothing. Although relieved that Daniel had a girlfriend, Helen felt somewhat disconcerted by the appearance of her daughter's new friends.

Later that evening, Emily called to ask if Jane was happy at the new school.

"She seems okay," said Helen. "Today she came home with a young man named Daniel who is eighteen, a seventeen-year-old girl named Rhiannon and Brendan, a sixteen-year-old with a safety pin through his eyebrow. All three of them were dressed in black."

"Really," said Emily. "I thought the Goth look had gone out of style. Remember years ago when Adam dyed his hair black and painted his nails. I used to cringe when he went to school wearing that ridiculous black trench coat and boots. He looked like a Nazi. I was so worried that his teachers would get the wrong impression and think that he was dangerous. He was such a good kid but he looked menacing. Jane's friends are probably nice kids too and will outgrow it, just as Adam did."

"Jane has told everyone at school that her name is Holly. Maybe she wants to dissociate herself from the girl who was bullied at Joan of Arc and went to jail. I guess she's just trying to make a fresh start. I can't really blame her after what's happened."

"Well, time will tell. May I say hello to Jane"

Helen handed the phone to Jane.

"Hi Auntie Em, I love going to Allerton High. I can wear what I want and the kids are nice. My friend Daniel is awesome. I had a cut on my leg and he licked the blood off of it."

"Oh!" said Emily. "I hope he isn't a vampire."

"Well, he kind of is. He sleeps in a coffin and belongs to the Vampire website."

"I'm glad you're happy at the new school Jane. Could you put your mom on now, please."

"Helen," said Emily, "I wish Jane could meet some kids her own age. Daniel sounds very immature for an eighteen-year-old. And why is he interested in a fourteen-year-old girl anyway?"

"Well, Rhiannon is his girlfriend. He and Jane are just classmates and if he makes her happy, I'm okay with the friendship. She needs friends. I can't be with her all the time and I'm worried that she might harm herself if left alone. Besides, other parents may not want their sons and daughters to associate with a girl who spent two weeks in jail. People may see Jane as undesirable. I'm just glad that some kids want her as a friend."

"Surely everything that happened to Jane is confidential and other parents and kids will never know."

"Don't be so naïve Emily. Of course they'll know. The police told Beth's family and Mr. Monardo, the principal of St. Joan of Arc. Teenagers are always chatting on MSN and Beth Henderson probably has hundreds of friends on Facebook. She's bound to know some of the kids who attend Allerton High. And maybe Mr. Monardo has called the new school. Absolutely nothing is confidential these days."

23.

PTSD and Panic Attacks

Helen finished typing a transcript after dinner and went to bed early. Totally exhausted and drifting into a luxurious deep sleep, she was suddenly jolted awake by Sandy jumping onto her bed then screams coming from Jane's bedroom. She rushed into her daughter's room and found her huddled in a corner shaking and moaning. She was sweating and looked terrified.

"Leave me alone!" she shouted. "Get away from me!"

Helen put her arms around her daughter but there was no recognition in Jane's eyes as she violently pushed her mother away. She appeared to be semi-conscious and reliving a terrifying event. Then, Sandy licked her face and she climbed back into bed. Helen sat stroking her daughter's hair and rubbing her back until she settled down. The following morning neither Jane nor her mother mentioned what had happened. Over the following months these night terrors became a regular occurrence. Helen wondered if they would plague her daughter for the rest of her life.

On Thursday evening Helen was pleased when she arrived home to find Jane and her three friends watching TV. Maybe life is going to be normal now, she thought hopefully.

"Mrs. Collins, tomorrow is a PA day. Can Holly go to a movie with us in the afternoon?" asked Daniel.

"No, I'm sorry, she can't," sighed Helen, realizing that life was not going to be normal for Jane until her draconian bail conditions were changed.

On Friday, Helen and James went to work and Jane stayed in the house all day with only Sandy, Jynx and Felix for company. As soon as her mother arrived home, she begged her to allow Trevor to come for a weekend visit. Helen decided that this might be a good idea. At least he was the same age as Jane. Then she remembered. "Jane," she sighed, "I'm afraid you will need to ask Trevor to write a note giving his permission for you to communicate with him. This was one of the bail conditions that we agreed to follow."

Jane explained to Trevor that they could not go to the movies or McDonald's because she was not allowed to enter the town of Toxteth.

"Even if your mother comes with us? Wow Holly, that's crazy," he said.

Jane and Trevor spent most of Saturday indoors watching TV and playing video games. In the afternoon, Helen took them out to walk Sandy in the local park. She felt as though she were in a time warp and once again had toddlers who could not venture outside unaccompanied.

Early Sunday morning Helen was awakened by a knock on her bedroom door. It was Trevor. "Mrs. Collins, I'm scared. There's something wrong with Holly," he said.

Helen grabbed her housecoat and went into the living room where she found her daughter looking alarmingly pale and gasping for air. She looked terrified.

"Mom, my heart has been beating really fast all night and it's getting harder to breathe. I can't get enough air. I'm really scared," she panted.

Helen threw on some clothes and the three rushed to a walk-in clinic where Jane was seen by a Dr. Devon who explained that she was suffering from a severe panic attack. He prescribed some medication and cautioned Helen that, in his opinion, her daughter was under too much stress to attend school for a few days. He recommended that she rest at home. Jane stayed home on Monday and Tuesday but was well enough to attend school for the remainder of the week.

On Friday afternoon, she and her mother went to pay Dr. Feldman a visit at Southern Ontario Hospital. Although Helen never wanted to set foot inside this hospital again and certainly did not want her daughter to be seen by anyone in the mental health unit, she felt obligated to keep one last appointment with Dr. Feldman since this was mentioned in the bail conditions.

Mother and daughter wiped their feet on the mat, one last time, and entered Dr. Feldman's office. Helen angrily told him that Tracey Hogan had given Jane's personal health information to the police, resulting in her being arrested, charged with uttering a threat, jailed for two weeks and now being a prisoner in her home. The doctor looked astonished and leaned back in his chair. He knew that Tracey would not have been permitted to do such a thing without first consulting with the hospital mental health team and that the ultimate decision to involve the police would have come from the Clinical Director, a psychiatrist named Dr. Joanne Simpson. He suspected that this doctor had directed Tracey Hogan to call the police without ever having met Jane herself but rather, relied upon details provided to her.

"They reported my patient to the police," he said incredulously. "Why wasn't I consulted? Didn't they know that she was my patient?"

After his initial reaction, the doctor composed himself and made an effort to support the decision. Helen took her daughter and left his office in disgust. "Well, Jane," she said. "You now have my permission to discontinue seeing Dr. Feldman."

On Saturday, Helen was exhausted after a grueling week of commuting back and forth to Newton. It was an eighty kilometre round trip and she was simply tired of driving. She just wanted to stay in Allerton and type transcripts for the day since she would be driving to Overton on Sunday to celebrate Jack's birthday at his sister Grace's house. Jane and her new friend, Brendan, seemed content playing video games and watching TV. Then there was a knock on the bedroom door.

"Mrs. Collins, do you mind if Holly and I take the bus into Newton to go to the Mall?" asked Brendan.

Helen of course did not want to tell him that her daughter was under house arrest, so she said, "Well, I was planning to do some shopping myself, so I'll drive you both to the Mall." She made an effort to smile.

The small family always gathered together for birthdays. Usually they met at Jack and Emily's home in Toronto, but this time, the celebration was being held at the home of Jack's younger sister Grace and her partner Ed who lived in Overton with their two cats and a friendly black dog named Ray Ban.

"How is Jane making out," asked Jack as they sat in the sun-room while Mark and Jane took Ray Ban for a walk.

Helen described her daughter's behaviour on the night when she seemed to be reliving a frightening event and could not be comforted.

"Oh no," said Jack's sister, Josie. "That sounds like post-traumatic stress disorder. I saw a TV program about it recently. It often affects soldiers returning home from war and can be a lifelong affliction. I wish Jane could get some help."

"Well she can't get help now. She would never trust a therapist after what has happened," Helen replied.

Just then, Grace's smiling face appeared in the doorway. "Would anyone like a drink?" she asked cheerfully.

24.

Holly and Daniel

Upon arriving home from work Monday evening, Helen was delighted to find Daniel, Brendan and Rhiannon watching TV with Jane. Encouraged, and hopeful that her daughter would establish a nice circle of friends, she invited the three to stay for dinner.

Tuesday was different. The house seemed strangely quiet when she walked in the door, and peeping into Jane's bedroom, she was shocked to discover Daniel sprawled across the bed. "Hi Mrs. Collins," he said with a sheepish grin.

"Where is your girlfriend, Rhiannon?" asked Helen shakily.

"I broke up with Rhiannon. Holly is my new girlfriend. She's just in the washroom now, colouring her hair," answered Daniel, smiling pleasantly.

Although Helen was dismayed when a raven-haired Jane emerged from the bathroom wearing heavy black eyeliner, reminiscent of King Tut, she did not make an issue of it. She wanted her daughter to be happy and have friends.

Thursday, October 5, 2006 was an important day in the life of Chris Collins. It was graduation day for the grade twelve students of St. Joan of Arc Catholic High School and Chris was not only graduating with honours but had won the Queen Elizabeth II award for excellence and a grant for having top marks. His proud family met at the school to witness the event; everyone but his sister Jane, who was not allowed to enter the town of Toxteth. Emily had asked Mark to stay at the house with Jane and keep her company.

It was a proud moment for Helen as she watched her son receive his diploma and scholarships. Mr. Monardo shook Chris' hand and posed with him as Emily stood in front of the stage and took photos of her nephew. When she sat down, her sister pointed out the Henderson family seated near the front of the auditorium. Beth Henderson, her parents and two stocky brothers hooted and clapped loudly for the eldest brother, Bill, a football player who had won a sports award.

After the ceremony, as the graduates and their families ate finger food and sipped coffee, Mr. Monardo spotted Helen in the crowd. As he rushed over to offer congratulations, he recognized Stephen, Jack and Emily. Mr. Monardo had been the vice-principal of St. Monica High School in Toronto a few years earlier and remembered meeting with Emily and Jack to discuss special programming for Stephen. "Well hello Mr. and Mrs. Morrison. How is Stephen doing," he asked as he shook their hands but ignored Stephen, who was standing with his parents.

"He is doing very well, thank you. Aren't you Stephen," replied Emily, turning to acknowledge her son and holding his alphabet board for him to communicate.

"YES I AM IN AN ADULT LITERACY PROGRAM. ITS NOT VERY CHALLENGING BUT I ENJOY USING THE COMPUTER. JANE SHOULD BE HERE," typed Stephen.

Mr. Monardo shrugged and, turning to Jack, asked, "Which of the graduates are you with?"

"We're here with our nephew Chris Collins," Jack answered proudly. "He is living with us now while he attends Seneca College."

"Chris has done very well indeed. He is a credit to his mother and I'm sure he will do well at Seneca. He is a hard working young man." said Mr. Monardo.

"We are also Jane Collins aunt and uncle," added Emily with a smile.

When the family returned to the house in Allerton, Emily saw that it had been unnecessary for Mark to have stayed with Jane. He, Jane and Daniel were seated together on the couch watching a movie. During the drive home to Toronto, he commented that Jane would always be Jane to him and never Holly.

When Helen called home during her coffee break on Friday, James gave her some disturbing news.

"I hate to tell you this Mom," he began, "but a cop called here looking for Jane. He phoned back and left a message for you, so maybe you should listen to your voice mail."

"Oh no, I hope Jane hasn't been skipping school. The police could arrest her for breaching her bail conditions and take her into custody."

"Well, I haven't seen her Mom."

Helen listened to her message. An Officer London advised that her daughter was missing from school and asked that she return his call. Her heart pounded as she phoned the number.

"Hello Mrs. Collins, I don't want to alarm you but we have been unable to locate Holly at Allerton High School and someone has been threatening to harm her."

It took a few moments for Helen to process this information. The officer had said that Holly had been threatened and was missing from school. He was not phoning because Jane had breached her bail conditions. In fact, he may not be aware that Holly and Jane were one and the same. She guessed that Rhiannon was upset about Daniel and had said something at school. Perhaps the guidance counsellor or principal had become concerned and phoned the police.

"Oh I'm sure it's nothing officer," said Helen with relief. "I will call the school just to make sure that Holly is there, but I don't think it's necessary to act on an offhand comment made by a child at school. Kids often say things they don't really mean. I think you should drop it. I will phone you if there is a real problem."

Helen called the school and spoke to her daughter. She cautioned Jane never to leave school property during the day then asked if she had been threatened.

"Well, yeah. Rhiannon said that she wants to kill me because I stole Daniel from her. She wrote "Daniel is a pedophile" on my locker and smeared boogers all over it. Daniel helped me to clean it off. I'm sorry that I left school at lunch time, Mom, but I was afraid of Rhiannon. I promise I won't do it again."

When Helen arrived home from work that evening; the delicious aroma of beef stew came wafting out of the kitchen, a sure sign that Joe, who loved to cook, was home for the weekend.

"Have a seat Mom," he said with a smile. "Dinner is almost ready. James went to work and Chris is at a party in Toxteth, so it will just be the three of us. I'll call Jane in a minute. She's in her bedroom doing homework." Then he leaned over and whispered, "A guy named Winston phoned long distance from Toronto and asked for Jane. I told him he had the wrong number."

After dinner, Helen retreated into her bedroom to type transcripts for the weekend. Seating herself at the desk, she turned on the transcriber and computer and noted that her treadmill was in need of a good dusting. Since Jane's troubles had begun, the previous June, it had fallen into disuse. Helen was now taking medication for high blood pressure and her cardiologist had warned that exercise was vital. But she felt too tired and depressed to care.

On the eighteenth of October, Mr. Moore felt obligated to phone Holly's mother to warn that an eighteen-year-old "Goth" youth had befriended her daughter. Helen replied that she was aware of the friendship and had no objections since she had met the young man and was satisfied that he was harmless. She indicated that Daniel was polite, did not smoke, drink or take drugs and seemed to be a very young eighteen. She could not tell the Vice-Principal of the school that Jane was under house arrest and that Daniel was the only student willing to spend time indoors with her instead of going out. She did not want Mr. Moore to know that Jane was nervous, depressed, and possibly suicidal. Helen found comfort in knowing that her daughter would not be alone in the house after school.

The following week, when she called home at coffee break time, James told her that Jane had been skipping classes lately and coming home during the day.

"I hate to rat on my sister," he said, "but, I'm worried about her. She comes running into the house in a panic, shuts herself in her room and goes to sleep. She says that Rhiannon is threatening her at school because she stole Daniel. Remember when Beth was bullying her for the same reason? Everyone picks on the poor kid. But something should be done about Rhiannon, Mom. She has been telling Jane that she plans to stab her. I saw her sitting at the top of our street last week and she was there again yesterday."

On October 26th, Helen phoned Officer London and suggested that perhaps the police should speak to Rhiannon and her parents. This seemed to solve the problem. However, another issue arose that day.

25.

A Fresh Start

Helen arrived home from work to find Jane crying in her bedroom with Sandy by her side. Daniel had gone home. "Mom, Mr. Moore called me into his office today," she said, hugging her dog.

"Was it about Rhiannon?"

"No. It was about Mr. Monardo from St. Joan of Arc calling my new school to warn Mr. Moore about me."

"What did Mr. Monardo tell him?"

"He told him that I had been bullied at St. Joan of Arc but that I was a bully too. Me! Why would he lie like that Mom?"

"I don't know Jane. What did Mr. Moore say to you?"

"He said that he didn't believe the part about me being a bully and he wants me to let him know if anyone ever bothers me at Allerton High. He's a nice man. I hope Mr. Monardo didn't tell him that I was in jail."

October 27, 2006

Mr. M. Monardo
St. Joan of Arc Catholic School
15 Glenwarren Road

Toxteth, ON L4P 2W6

Dear Mr. Monardo,

My daughter Jane Collins did not have a very positive experience in grades 7 and 8 at St. Joan. Last year in particular she was horribly bullied constantly throughout the latter part of the year on MSN and on school property. I have enclosed a sample of some of the MSN bullying from other students who also attended St. Joan.

I wanted Jane to have a good, fresh start at Allerton High School. The staff and students there are very considerate and Jane has already made quite a few nice friends.

I was, therefore, extremely disappointed to learn from Jane that you had contacted Mr. Moore, the Vice-Principal of Allerton High, and told him that, not only was my daughter bullied at your school, but that she was a bully too. This is not true. Jane has never bullied anyone and I think it was inexcusable for you to have made such a comment to Mr. Moore at her new school.

I would like you to write a letter to Mr. Moore retracting that statement and I would also like you to copy Jane on that letter apologizing for making such a comment.

I look forward to your reply.

Yours truly,

Helen Collins

Enclosure

Mr. Monardo phoned Helen and expressed annoyance. He did not write a letter or contact Mr. Moore by telephone.

26.

CAS and CAMH

The Children's Aid Society was on Jane's case and Helen understood that it was perilous to ignore them. Having worked in Family Court, she was aware of the power that this organization wielded. They sometimes made serious mistakes by either targeting the wrong families or ignoring those that needed intervention. When they called and insisted on meeting with Jane, Helen had no choice but to comply. So, after missing many days of school due to her detention and the resulting panic attacks, Jane was required to miss another day in order to be interrogated by the CAS.

On Friday, the twentieth of October, a young man named Peter came to the house and introduced himself as a CAS worker. Helen offered him coffee and cookies. As he sipped his coffee, Peter explained that Steve Cook, a crisis worker at Southern Ontario Hospital, had notified the CAS of a possible case of child abuse by Jane's father, Greg Collins. Jane said that she had not meant to say those things to Steve and wished she could retract them.

Helen admitted it had been an error in judgment to have allowed her daughter to spend a weekend with Greg, whom she had not seen in several years. She assured Peter that, after meeting him, Jane did not wish to see her father again, but that neither she nor Jane believed charges against Greg were warranted. She indicated that her daughter had many issues to deal with and adding one more problem might be too much for her. Tracey Hogan's betrayal of Jane's confidence was explained to him. To her surprise, Peter was sympathetic to her plight and expressed outrage that a crisis counsellor had contacted the police to report a young victim of bullying. Helen told him that one of the girls who had bullied Jane was Nadia Reeves, a CAS client according to Ms. Hogan. She advised him that they had been informed, by Tracey, of Nadia's involvement with Rita, a CAS case worker. Peter took notes and advised Helen and Jane that the CAS would be investigating Tracey Hogan for breach of confidentiality. He shook their hands and gave his assurance that the file involving allegations of child abuse would be closed.

On Friday, October 27th Helen was required to forfeit a day's pay since Jane had been ordered by the court to miss another day of school and submit to an assessment at the Centre for Addiction and Mental Health. Jane had been so frightened and anxious about the assessment that Helen agreed to allow Daniel to join them. "Don't worry Holly, I'll be waiting right outside," he assured her.

It was a long journey from Allerton to CAMH in Toronto and Helen dreaded having to drive in the city. Parking was expensive and she was unfamiliar with that particular area of Toronto. She was also extremely apprehensive about Jane being forced to speak to a mental health professional, and believed the entire exercise to be unnecessary and punitive. It made her angry to think of how much the system had punished her daughter, and continued to do so.

Jill Witmer was just as Helen had imagined, an eager, officious psychologist with a knowing smile. Jill explained to Helen and Jane that she would be doing clinical interviews with Jane during the first day and cognitive and academic testing on subsequent days. Helen had decided to delay future testing for as long as possible in the hope that the Crown would see reason and withdraw the charge, rendering it unnecessary.

Jill interviewed Jane and Helen separately. Both resented being subjected to such a humiliating process and found it intrusive and frightening. Helen believed that everything they said could be twisted by psychologists to suit their own purposes. Naturally, they would believe that everyone who entered CAMH would require some sort of counselling. It was what they did.

Jane was terrified of Jill Witmer. It had been her experience that people such as Jill wielded a great deal of power over her and she did not want more bad things to happen as a result of saying the wrong thing. When Jill smiled at her, Jane felt so nervous and sick that she had difficulty breathing and feared vomiting, fainting or a major panic attack. She struggled to appear calm. Jill asked about her life history, current situation and future goals and Jane answered promptly.

Jill noted in her report, *"Jane presented with flat affect, did not readily engage in small talk with the examiner, and did not smile during the interview. She appeared to understand the purpose of this assessment although she appeared somewhat confused about her charges."*

Under the heading of *"Circumstances surrounding Charges,"* Jill noted the following: *"Jane explained that the charges resulted from her telling a crisis counsellor her fantasies about harming a bully. Jane did not deny that she had told her counsellor about plans to kidnap and kill a female peer, Beth, who had bullied her. However, she explicitly denied that she intended to actually harm the other girl. Jane believed it was obvious to others that she was not an aggressive person or physically capable of committing such an act. She admitted that she stole the scenario from a horror movie. She believed that Ms. Hogan had encouraged her to share her fantasies as part of the thera-*

peutic process. Ms. Hogan was not interviewed as part of this assessment because Jane and her mother refused to consent to the interviewer contacting Ms. Hogan. However, given that Ms. Hogan contacted the police regarding Jane's threats we can infer that Ms. Hogan had very significant concerns that Jane would follow through on her fantasies."

When asked about truancy, Jane admitted that she had sometimes skipped classes in order to avoid Daniel's former girlfriend, Rhiannon, who had been threatening to harm her. She was confused when Jill asked if she recognized a similarity between this situation and the previous situation with Beth. She mulled this over in her mind. Beth and Matt broke up, she thought. Beth talked Nadia into threatening me so she wouldn't get into trouble. I never threatened Beth and when the police asked her about it, Beth told them that I never threatened her and that things were okay between us. All I did was to tell Tracey that I was mad at Beth. But when Daniel and Rhiannon broke up, she really did threaten me. She messed up my locker and said that she was going to stab me. She was waiting for me at the top of my street. James saw her, a couple of times. So, I never threatened Beth. It was only in my mind. But Rhiannon threatened me to my face. So one was just a thought and the other was real.

"No, it wasn't the same thing at all," Jane concluded.

Jill wrote in her report: *"Jane admitted to poor school attendance during the first few months at her new school. She said it was because she was avoiding her boyfriend's ex-girlfriend. When the similarities between her current situation with her new boyfriend and his ex-girlfriend and the events leading up to her charges were pointed out to Jane, she did not have any understanding or insight around why this girl was bothering her or what she should do about it. Jane's only strategy for dealing with the conflict was to skip school and avoid the other girl."*

"Both Jane and her mother believed that the counselling at Southern Ontario Hospital was supposed to help Jane with her

anxiety and peer issues. However, Jane felt that her anxiety was not addressed and did not feel the sessions were helpful. When asked about her feelings towards Ms. Hogan, Jane said she did not like her and that she considered her a liar. Jane was not comfortable with us contacting Ms. Hogan as part of this assessment. Jane did not seem able to separate her feelings about the helpfulness of therapy from her anger toward the therapist."

"When asked what needs to change in order to help her socially and emotionally, Jane said she needs to have the court process behind her and to have her bail restrictions lifted so that she can resume her life. Overall, Jane felt it would be very difficult for her to trust a counsellor again. She felt that before this incident she was more trusting. She explained that her close friends had turned against her and she felt Ms. Hogan had turned against her as well."

After her interview with Helen, Jill Witmer wrote the following in her report:

"Ms. Collins spoke about her reaction to her daughter's charge during our interview. She believed that if she had not sought counselling for Jane and encouraged her daughter to share all of her feelings, Jane would not be in this current situation. Ms. Collins did not understand the charge and was particularly angry about the 14 days that Jane had to spend in custody due to a bail error. She believed that if her daughter had mental health issues that jail was the last place she should have been sent. Ms. Collins described her daughter as dramatic and as a youth with a good imagination who likes to write poems and stories. She felt that Jane was likely flattered that Ms. Hogan wanted to listen to her creative story about Beth. Ms. Collins did not believe that her daughter would be capable of hurting Beth or any person. She explained that her daughter is passive and has no previous history of peer conflict or aggression."

Although Jill had been made aware that Jane was a prisoner in her home due to her bail conditions, she wrote the following in her report: *"Jane is not in any organized activities; however, she enjoys music, reading and writing poetry. Overall Jane's leisure time is generally spent with her boyfriend or in solitary activities and appears to lack structure."*

After having Jane complete a number of tests, Jill concluded that *"Jane did not report clinically significant problems with either anger or aggression."*

Relieved that the first day of testing was over, Helen treated Jane and Daniel to an early dinner at Swiss Chalet then wearily fought her way home to Allerton through rush hour traffic.

Although it was supposedly an important assessment ordered by a judge, Jill Witmer did not always take the time to confirm the accuracy of details noted in her report. She stated *"Jane was diagnosed with an Anxiety Disorder, Obsessive-Compulsive Disorder and an Eating Disorder at Toronto Hospital."* Helen advised Ms. Witmer that this information was false but it was never removed from her report. Ultimately, however, it was of no consequence since only three people took the time to read the completed document, Helen, Emily and Jack.

27.

Proceed by Indictment

"When I was young," said Emily, "kids stopped celebrating Halloween long before high school. I remember feeling silly going door to door wearing a cowgirl costume when I was twelve. Things are different now. A few years ago, when Adam was seventeen, he went out for Trick-or-Treat dressed as Marilyn Manson. Mark is planning to dress as Jack Skellington, a *Nightmare Before Christmas* character. He won't be going door to door though. He's been invited to a party."

"Yes, everyone celebrates Halloween now, even adults," replied Helen, "but not Jane. Since she isn't allowed out of the house without me, she plans to paint her face and give out candy at the door."

"It doesn't make sense," sighed Emily. "She has been incarcerated now for nearly two months. One of my co-workers at Canada Revenue Agency was convicted of stealing $270,000 from the government and was sentenced to only three months house arrest with no jail time."

On October 31st Jack Skellington went to a Halloween party with a group of friends. Sally, the doll with the stitched face, stayed home with her mother and answered the door to Trick-or-Treaters.

The following day, Mike Rivers attended court on Jane's behalf and was astonished when advised that the Crown attorney, Lynne Thomas, had decided the case would proceed by Indictment. This meant that Jane was required to be present at each court date and if she failed to do so, a bench warrant would be issued for her arrest unless a lawyer had been designated to appear on her behalf.

Helen was shocked that Lynne Thomas had decided to proceed by Indictment. She was aware that only the most serious criminal cases, such as those involving murder, acts of terrorism, treason, drug trafficking and other such serious crimes were dealt with in this manner. Most cases, including some types of rape, were Summary Convictions. It seemed to Helen that Lynne Thomas was not a reasonable, rational person. It was she who had made the decision not to grant bail to Jane under any circumstances despite the fact that there should always be a presumption of bail in cases involving children and youth. Young people were rarely held in custody.

"What do you know about Lynne Thomas?" Emily asked her sister after Helen had explained what was meant by an Indictable Offense.

"She recently got married and is expecting a baby," replied Helen.

"Well, isn't that sweet," said Emily sarcastically. "I guess she's young and inexperienced."

"No, she wouldn't be a Crown attorney if she were inexperienced."

"Then I don't understand. Why is it an Indictable Offence? Since when, is it a heinous crime to ask for help at a hospital?"

"I don't understand either. About ninety percent of all cases are Summary Convictions. Only the most horrific crimes are Indictable Offenses."

On November 15th, the next court date, Helen took no chances and brought Jane to the courthouse, so worried was she that her daughter could be arrested if her lawyer failed to make an appearance. Upon seeing Jane, Mike Rivers advised that it would be unnecessary for her to miss any more school time. He assured Helen that either he or someone from his office would be at the court on the appointed days. As it turned out, there were many.

It became obvious to Helen that it would be necessary for Jane to complete the CAMH assessment. She pleaded with Jill Witmer to do the cognitive and academic testing in one long day instead of two and Jill agreed. Jane, therefore, was absent from school on November 24th for the purpose of this testing. The results were compiled by Jill who completed her report on December 11, 2006. It was filed in the "pre-sentencing report" drawer and copies were given to the Crown attorney, judge and defence lawyer. Helen doubted that any of them would actually read the lengthy report.

Mike attended court on Jane's behalf on November 22nd, November 29th, December 13th, December 14th, December 15th and December 18th. After the December 18th appearance, which was a pre-trial conference before Justice Bloom, Mr. Rivers wrote a letter to Jane to advise her of an offer made by the Crown attorney who had come from the town of Bantry. He explained that the charge would be withdrawn on January 16, 2007 if she agreed to enter into a section 810 recognizance with the following conditions:

- no communication with Beth Henderson;
- not attend at or near her place of residence, employment or education;
- attend school; and
- attend counselling and provide written proof to Crown of same.

Mr. Rivers went on to explain that a section 810 recognizance was a peace bond. He assured Jane that she would not be required to admit any wrongdoing and it was not a criminal record. He recommended acceptance of this offer since it was a guaranteed result.

When Jane read Mike's letter, her heart pounded rapidly and she began to tremble and hyperventilate. "I'm not going to speak to another counsellor!" she gasped. "And a peace bond sounds scary!"

"You don't have to do anything, sweetheart. Take deep breaths and try to calm down," said Helen as she rushed to get Jane's medication.

As a Court Reporter, Helen knew that a permanent police record would be created if her daughter were to sign a peace bond. It would follow her for the rest of her life and create difficulties when she applied for employment. It would also mean that a police officer would visit the Henderson family to assure them that Jane had signed such a document. This was unacceptable to Jane and Helen, who sent the following response letter:

Re: Jane Collins Court Appearance – January 16, 2007

On January 16, 2007, Jane Collins will not be signing the S.810 peace bond. Please ask the Crown to withdraw the charge as no crime was committed. Remind them that this was a child venting to a counsellor about her feelings and she thought she was doing so in confidence. That's what counselling is all about. As the CAMH report states, Jane was never a threat to anyone. Jane deserves an apology from all parties concerned.

If for some reason you are unable to convince them to drop the charge and it goes to trial, we want these harsh bail conditions amended as follows:

1. Delete condition 4, house arrest curfew
2. Amend condition 8, not attend the Town of Toxteth

We are planning to attend court on the 16th if necessary. Please advise.

Yours truly,

Jane Collins and Helen Collins

28.

Prisoners

Jane loved the holiday season. She enjoyed trimming the Christmas tree, shopping for presents and wrapping them in festive paper to be arranged under the tree. She loved baking Grandma's special Christmas cookies and mince tarts and building gingerbread houses with her mother. Christmas meant going to midnight mass at the church, family gatherings and parties with friends. Christmas 2006, however, was different. She could not go Christmas shopping unless accompanied by her mother. She was forced to decline party invitations and the family did not attend midnight mass. On Christmas day the entire family of fourteen gathered at the home of Emily and Jack.

"Jane why don't you play some Christmas carols on the piano like you did last year," suggested Auntie Em. Jane sat on the piano stool and placed her slim fingers on the keys. As everyone waited in anticipation, she suddenly spun around. "I'm sorry," she said. "It's been a long time since I've had music lessons and I have forgotten how to play. I know I could do it if I could just have Mr. Reynolds show me again. Mom, couldn't we just go to Toxteth for one more lesson?"

"You know the answer to that," replied Helen.

Since her mother and brothers worked between Christmas and New Year, Jane spent the holidays at home with Daniel and the pets for company. She and Daniel had been invited to a New Year's Eve party at the home of a school friend. "You don't have to stay home with me Daniel," said Jane. "I'll be okay. You can go to Kayla's party and tell me about it tomorrow."

"It wouldn't be any fun without you Holly. I'll stay here and we can watch TV and make popcorn," replied Daniel chivalrously.

Helen was in a rigid, stressful routine that allowed no time for herself. She dare not stop on the way home from work to shop or have coffee with friends. She declined all evening invitations since her daughter needed her. Every day she raced home to Allerton knowing that Jane and Daniel would be waiting for her to take them out of the house. So desperate was Jane to go out, that neither the destination nor the activity mattered. She was eager to accompany her mother to the grocery store, the Laundromat or even to Jiffy Lube to get an oil change for the car. She felt restless and claustrophobic at home, and Helen was trapped spending all of her free time with two teenagers. These mind numbing days spread out ahead of her, interminably, each one the same as the last. She worked at the courthouse, drove home, entertained Jane and Daniel and then typed transcripts in her bedroom. No longer did she use her treadmill nor have any interest in reading or watching television. She was depressed and blamed herself for all that had befallen her daughter. Her blood pressure soared and she was not eating or sleeping properly. Dr. March warned that recent blood tests had revealed that she was on the verge of developing Diabetes as a result of poor diet, lack of exercise and stress and that extreme stress could cause her blood sugar to spike.

Emily and Jack were gravely concerned about Helen and Jane, but felt powerless to help. It seemed that the justice system was conspiring to inflict as much damage, pain and suffering on them as possible. Our tax dollars at work, thought Jack angrily.

On January 16th Helen and Jane went to the courthouse as it would be necessary for them to sign the new bail conditions should they be changed. Helen remembered Justice Bloom's promise to relax the conditions and felt optimistic that he would do so. Mike Rivers was busy with a trial in Toronto and had sent an attorney named Don Rossi to represent Jane. Don was an idealistic young lawyer who found the case to be cruel and unjust. To his surprise, he was unsuccessful in his bid to have the harsh bail conditions changed as Jane and Helen had requested. In refusing to do so Justice Bloom indicated that it was no longer within his jurisdiction. Jane and Helen felt bitter and betrayed yet again. As they drove home to Allerton, Jane did not cry, but sat stoically beside her mother. "I can't live like this. I wish I were dead," Helen heard her daughter whisper to herself.

Subsequent to the March 8th pre-trial, Mike sent a letter dated March 19, 2007 to Jane and Helen. The Crown was no longer insisting that Jane sign a peace bond. She need only agree to go for counselling and the charge would be withdrawn. Mike strongly recommended that Jane become involved with a counsellor who could provide him with a good report. He indicated that this was a guaranteed good resolution that would not be too difficult to comply with. Jane disagreed. She adamantly refused to meet with a counsellor. A trial date was set for May 31st.

Most of the students and staff at Allerton High School had been looking forward to March Break vacation week. Some had planned cruises or flights to the sunny south, while others would be staying home and perhaps going on day trips. Helen and James were unable to take holidays during the break. Chris and Joe were busy with their studies and Daniel was working with his father to earn some extra money. March Break at Mark's school in Toronto was held later in the month. Jane spent the holiday alone in the house with her pets, watching television and playing solitary video games. She was relieved when it was over and she was allowed to leave the house and return to school.

Shortly after the break, as she walked down the corridor of Allerton High School, Jane recognized a student from St. Joan of Arc coming toward her. As she attempted to duck into a classroom, a voice called out to her and she knew it was futile to hide.

"Hi Jane, what's up?" asked Tiffany Marks.

"Oh hi Tiff. How come you're in my school?"

"Basketball game. Hey, have you seen Beth Henderson? She's been looking all over for you."

"Um no. Well, got to go. Late for class," said Jane breathlessly as she ran down the hallway, around the corner and out the front door. She ran and ran and did not stop running until she was safely at home in her bedroom.

"That was a close call," she said to Sandy. "If Beth had found me, the police would have taken me away. I'm not supposed to be anywhere near her."

When Helen arrived home from work, she found Jane huddled in bed with Sandy. "Oh Mom, I'm not safe anywhere," she cried. "Beth was at my school today. I think I should stay home until my trial day. I don't want to go back to jail."

Helen explained to her daughter that the bail conditions only meant that she was not to go to the town of Toxteth and that it was not her concern if Beth happened to be at her school in Allerton.

"Lucky Beth," said Jane. "She can go anywhere she wants."

29.

The Trial

It was the thirty-first of May, 2007. Jane and her mother climbed the stairs to the second floor of the courthouse with grave trepidation. This was it. The long anticipated trial date had arrived. There was a cruel shock awaiting Jane on the other side of the door. As they opened it, she gasped and jumped back into the stairwell.

"Oh no, oh no," she whispered to Helen as she flattened herself against the wall. "It's her! Beth Henderson is sitting right outside the courtroom with her mother. Why is she here?"

Helen thought for a moment. "Well, the only explanation I can think of, Jane, is that the Crown attorney didn't read your case in advance and thought that Beth was needed as a witness."

"But I never threatened her. This isn't about her," cried Jane. "Now she's going to go back to her school and tell everyone about this. It's not fair. The kids will all make fun of me."

"Don't worry Jane. She won't be called as a witness. It's just a mistake. Hold your head up high and ignore Beth. She doesn't go to your school anyway. Who cares what the kids in Toxteth think."

"I do," said Jane.

Helen was livid. Countless mistakes had been made by uncaring people resulting in so many indignities suffered by her daughter. "We can't stay in the stairwell Jane," she said, opening the door. Look, there's Uncle Jack and Auntie Em waiting for us behind Beth. Let's go and sit with them.

"There's Tracey, sitting with that evil cop," said Jane. "It looks like she's listening to something. She's wearing head-phones."

Emily was surprised when she first laid eyes on Tracey Hogan. Jack looked askance. Helen had pointed her out when she and Jane joined them. Tracey was not, as Emily had imag-ined, an attractive young woman with a confident smile, nor was she a dowdy older woman as Jack had thought. No, the fortyish woman, chatting with Detective Rutledge, looked truly wicked. Perfect, thought Emily as she regarded the thin angular face, the sallow skin, aquiline nose and long red hair. She wore a grim black suit with a frock coat.

"All she needs to complete the ensemble is a pointed hat and a broomstick," Emily whispered to her husband.

"I'm surprised Jane didn't take one look at that woman and run," muttered Jack. "She certainly doesn't look like a friendly approachable type of person. I can't imagine anyone confiding in her."

Jane worried about her appearance. She had chosen to wear a white long sleeved shirt and black pants to court, thinking that this would please the judge.

"Do I look okay Auntie Em?" she asked.

"You look perfect, Jane," answered Emily who had previously suggested to her that the black hair and eyeliner were not a good idea. Jane had lightened her hair closer to its natural colour but was wearing eyeliner to hide her lack of eyelashes. She had absent-mindedly plucked them all out when feeling worried and anxious.

As Beth Henderson and her mother sat with their backs to Jane and her family; Detective Rutledge approached them. The family heard him telling Beth that she was not needed and could collect her subpoena pay before leaving the courthouse. Clearly, Beth had been subpoenaed in error. Jane felt as though she had been sucker-punched in the stomach by the justice system, again.

Court would soon be in session and the family waited nervously in the courtroom. Jack, seated between Emily and Helen, held their shaky hands as he studied the Ontario Coat of Arms on the wall ahead. He was a good man, an upstanding citizen who had volunteered his time in the community for scouting and coaching children's hockey and baseball. He was a business owner and an honest taxpayer. Emily regarded the desolate expression on her husband's face. She had seen a similar look before, on her father's face when she had given him the terrible news that her mother, his beloved wife, had passed away. It was a look of pain and disbelief. Jack had completely lost faith in the Canadian justice system and feared for his young niece.

At length, the judge entered his courtroom followed by a clerk who announced, "Order! All rise. This Ontario Court of Justice is now in session, the Honourable Justice Christie presiding. Please be seated."

Crown Counsel, Ms. Parson, a stocky woman with close-cropped blonde hair, rose to her feet and called Tracey Hogan to the stand.

As Jane sat transfixed with fear, she glimpsed, through the corner of her eye, the black clothing of the sole crown witness as she swept up the aisle, and imagined her flying on a broomstick. The entrance music for the *Wicked Witch of the West* in the *Wizard of Oz* movie played in her young mind. A grim-faced Tracey Hogan stood at the front of the courtroom and swore to tell the truth. She looked down her long nose at the accused. *I'll get you...and your little dog too!* Jane imagined her threatening.

Ms. Parson smiled at her witness and asked, "How did Jane present herself to you at your first meeting?"

"Slight in stature, fragile in physical appearance, bandages from her knees down. She had used a large butcher knife to cut her legs from her kneecaps to her shins."

"And on what dates did you see Jane Collins?"

"June the 9th, August 3rd, August 14th and August 28th."

Jane turned and faced her mother. She was surprised that Tracey seemed to have forgotten their meeting at the school on August 16th and the appointment of August 18th. Helen shook her head and motioned for her daughter to turn around and face the judge. How unprofessional not to have made any clinical notes, she thought. It had been during the August 18th appointment that copies of the MSN bullying had been given to Tracey, who had then disclosed information about Nadia Reeves. She had provided an appointment card for August 28th with "Youthdale" and a phone number written on the back. Helen still had this card.

"And did you have any concerns that there may be a risk of harm to others at the August 3rd meeting?"

"Yes, I had concerns. She disclosed that she was having problems with her boyfriend whom she met at Toronto Hospital. I don't know for fact that that's where she actually was."

Helen was angry. She felt it misleading to refer to Trevor as Jane's "boyfriend." It gave the impression that he was much older and had a mature relationship with her daughter. She wanted to explain to the court that Trevor was a troubled thirteen-year-old boy who Jane had only happened to meet because Tracey Hogan had arranged to send her to Toronto Hospital for an unnecessary assessment. But, of course, she sat in silence.

"And did you have concerns on August 14th that Jane may harm others," continued Ms. Parson.

"Yes. Jane disclosed that her new boyfriend had become physically aggressive with her and chased her with a syringe that he used for injecting himself with Insulin and that she was very afraid. She disclosed that together with her boyfriend they were doing Ecstasy and..."

"I object Your Honour," interrupted Mike Rivers. "This is highly prejudicial. It is confidential communication between my client and a counsellor who is working in a mental health facility under the auspices of doctors and I don't think it is of any assistance."

"Alright," said Justice Christie, "I can take from the answer that there was a concern about the new boyfriend and that she was expressing some fears. It may be relevant but I don't think I need to hear too much more about the new relationship do I?"

"I think you do, Your Honour," answered Ms. Parson. "In terms of what the threat is, this may make it a bit clearer." Turning to the witness, she asked, "Did this information cause you concern?"

"Well yeah, absolutely. It lent my understanding as to what was motivating Jane to disclose to me that she was considering acting out against her boyfriend and why she was upset with him and also an ex-girlfriend."

"Was this an ex-girlfriend of the boyfriend or Jane?"

"It was a person that Jane had previously viewed as her friend but they had a falling out."

"Okay. Was that person named?"

"Beth. Named as Beth Henderson."

"And did Jane say that she's been thinking about killing the boyfriend and an ex-girlfriend?"

"Yes, we talked about that. She said that she was having suicidal thoughts because her boyfriend was angry with her. She disclosed that she and her boyfriend broke into a car."

Mike jumped to his feet. "Your Honour, I object. This just isn't relevant."

Justice Christie turned to Ms. Parson. "Help me here with this one Crown," he said.

"I think, Your Honour, it becomes relevant as to what this witness thinks is Jane's state of mind," she answered.

Helen, Emily and Jack had the same thought. Tracey Hogan was not qualified to judge Jane's state of mind. Dr. Feldman, who was qualified, did not believe that she was a threat to anyone. Jane regretted inventing stories to entertain Tracey.

"Just sort of backing up," continued Ms. Parson, "Jane said that she had been thinking about killing her boyfriend and an ex-girlfriend and that she broke into a car. Did that raise some concerns for you?"

"Yes, when I'm interviewing a child, I'm doing a mental status exam and I'm checking in what realm is the child functioning."

Jane was alarmed that Tracey had believed, without question, everything that she had said. She desperately wanted to tell Justice Christie that she had not broken into a car or stolen anything. Trevor had boasted about doing these things but she was certain that his stories were not true.

"I was concerned that Jane did not have control over her behavior," continued Tracey. "She disclosed to me that she had been starting fires, that she was burning leaves, paper, toys, books and herself."

"Burning herself?"

"Yes, she indicated that she had burned herself the previous day and that she had burned her medication bottle. I clearly remember that Jane did produce her medication bottle and it was melted."

Jane reproached herself for producing the melted medication bottle just to get a reaction from Tracey. The label showing Trevor Brown's name had been burned off. Emily smiled at her sister and shook her head. Helen rolled her eyes. Jack expected the Crown to ask Tracey if she had seen any burns on Jane herself, but she did not.

"And how does this relate to her telling you about her thoughts of killing her boyfriend and Beth Henderson?"

"I checked in with her, as I would any client who may be suicidal. We do a safety check if the child has disclosed some homicidal ideation. It's part of what we do as an outpatient program to ensure that the child is safe. And Jane indicated that she had been thinking about killing her boyfriend and an ex-girlfriend, Beth Henderson. She told me that she was thinking of slitting the corners of Beth's mouth and then sewing it back up. She indicated that she wanted to torture Beth, that she wanted to hang Beth, that she wanted to beat and electrocute her, and that she deserves to feel pain."

"How did you take what was said to you?"

"Quite seriously. We're a crisis program. We're in the business of mental health. Children who are ill come to us, so we take those kinds of things seriously."

Helen was angry. Her daughter was not ill. She was a normal teenager with a real problem of being bullied at school and online. Surely Tracey did not believe that a parent would take a mentally ill child to speak with a mere counsellor.

"Did she speak of any further harm to others?"

"There was another individual that was named. Jane said she wanted to hurt someone named Monica, with no surname. And she did actually say that she wouldn't kill Monica, just harm her. Also during that session, she told me that she wasn't planning to carry out her plan until September."

"What do you take this plan to be in reference to?"

"Jane told me that her plan was to abduct Beth and take her to an undisclosed field – I don't know where – in the back roads of Allerton and that's where she would slit the corners of her mouth and sew it back together and torture her. And she felt that she could abduct her at knifepoint. She told me that she had no intention of carrying out the plan until September. She states that she might get caught but would kill herself. I asked if she knew where Beth lived and she said yes, that she did."

"Why did you ask her that question?"

"I was trying to sort out the level of lethality involved in the plan."

"And at the end of the session, what view did you hold?"

"I consulted with a psychiatrist."

"And did you speak of your concerns with any other person connected with Jane Collins?"

"At that appointment, I don't believe that I had the opportunity to do that."

Helen wondered why none of these concerns had been mentioned to her when she joined Tracey and Jane at the end of the appointment.

"At the end of the session, did you have any concern of risk of harm to others?"

"I was concerned that Jane may potentially act out against her boyfriend or Beth or Monica. I was concerned for the other kids"

"I understand that the next time you spoke to Jane was August 28th. Is that correct?"

"Yes, I'm recalling that we set up an appointment for August 18th which would have been two appointments in the same week which is out of the realm of the norm…"

Helen shook her head. Well it may have been "out of the realm of the norm" she thought, but it happened.

"…it's different from the way we usually practice," continued Tracey with authority, "We usually see children once a week. At the time I was sufficiently concerned that I suggested meeting on the 18th, which would have been the Friday. I didn't meet with Jane on the 18th as I think she and her family had gone on a short holiday."

Jane wondered if Tracey had forgotten their August 18th appointment or was simply lying.

"And then I had holidays. When we go on vacation, we alert our colleagues. We also talk about community resources and invite people to attend our emergency department."

Yes, thought Helen. And on August 18th you gave me the name and phone number of Youthdale because you were going on holiday.

"So, just to confirm, Ms. Hogan, from August 14th, you did not see Jane Collins until August 28th?"

"That's correct."

"Okay. Then on August 28th did you have any concerns?"

"Yes, I checked in with her about the homicidality. She stated that she didn't plan to hurt Beth right now because she's not bugging her. She indicated that Beth wants to be her friend but she doesn't trust her. So there was evidence that there had been some contact between the two girls. Being summer, I was comforted by the fact that they lived in separate towns and access wasn't every day at school."

Helen wanted to shout out, "Then why did you tell me that switching schools would be a big mistake?" But of course she sat in silence.

"But it was new information that Beth had indicated she wanted to be friends. Jane said that if Beth bugged her, she would punch her in the face and consider following through with her plan. When I asked if she would really hurt Beth, she reported quite clearly that she would."

Jane made eye contact with her mother and shook her head. She clearly remembered Tracey had asked that question and she had responded, "No, I would just walk away."

"So, did you, as a result of your concerns, do something?"

"I consulted with one of our staff psychiatrists and I recommended, to Mrs. Collins, that she consider admitting her daughter to Youthdale."

Helen took deep breaths to calm herself. It took all of her strength and willpower not to shout out that Tracey had only mentioned Youthdale once, after the August 18th appointment. "If you have any problems with Jane while I'm on vacation, you can call this phone number and have her admitted to Youthdale," she had said.

"And why did you suggest Youthdale?"

"Because it wasn't possible to admit Jane to our hospital. When I consulted with the psychiatrist, that is what I was looking for."

"Did you make any suggestions to Mrs. Collins?"

"I suggested Youthdale. The following day I consulted with Dr. Simpson, the Clinical Director of our program because Jane was not admitted to our hospital. We have clinical supervision for three hours every Tuesday with the Director, who is a psychiatrist. And it was discussed at a team level. The team concluded that it would be my responsibility to consult with the police and to convey what had been disclosed. That I was to attempt to call Toronto Hospital to see if they had anything to offer because that's where Jane was sent and we hadn't received anything back from them. Typically when a child goes from our hospital to another, a report will follow the child back to us."

Helen suspected that a report had not been prepared because Dr. Cohen believed that Jane had been sent to Toronto Hospital in error and there was nothing to report about her mental condition. The doctor had said that Jane was a normal teenager who was under stress due to bullying.

Court recessed for lunch. As the family trooped across the street to McDonald's, a shaky Helen and Jane breathed in the fresh air and tried to calm themselves. Jane was so nervous that she was unable to eat the chicken nuggets and fries that her uncle Jack had bought for her and she refused the offer of a Smarties McFlurrie, her usual favourite. Helen drank her coffee despondently.

"It seems that everything Hogan says is accepted as the gospel truth," she moaned.

"I don't think the judge is impressed with her testimony," said Emily. "She's a terrible witness. I think she comes across as cold and uncaring. Her answers seem convoluted and designed to confuse."

"She should be in big trouble for lying to the judge," said Jane.

When court resumed, Ms. Parson continued her questioning and the family wearily hoped that the case would be resolved that afternoon.

"In looking at Jane Collins, Ms. Hogan, do you see any contrast or similarities between how she appeared last summer and how she appears today?"

When I met with Jane in June, she was significantly slighter than she is now. She seems to have gained some weight."

She thinks I look fat, thought Jane in dismay. Maybe I should try to diet down to ninety pounds again. It's not fair. I gained weight because I couldn't go outside for so many months.

"You mentioned that Jane seemed not to want to go back to school or wasn't too happy with school. Do you recall what she didn't like about school?"

"The school-related issues were primarily focused around the bullying that was going on at school. Jane was being bullied by other female students at school. And as I understand it, there was some reciprocation. Jane disclosed to me that she was suspended for telling a teacher – and I can swear, right – to fuck off. I'm not comfortable saying that, but that is what it was, as I understood it. Jane felt unsupported by the school."

"And after August 28th, did you ever counsel Jane again?"

"No."

"Thank you. Those are my questions. If you could stay there, His Honour may have some and Mr. Rivers will have some questions for you."

"Right," said his Honour. "Mr. Rivers, ready to proceed?

"Yes I am. Thank you Your Honour," answered Mike as he rose to his feet and approached the witness with a tight smile on his red face.

Jane breathed a sigh of relief as she regarded her lawyer admiringly. She thought him handsome and formidable in his dark suit and tie. "Please force Tracey to tell the truth," she muttered under her breath.

"In total, how many times did you see Jane?" Mike began. "The reason I ask is because you told Detective Rutledge that you saw her six meetings in total. Is that correct?"

"Yes, I did say that on the tape that I listened to this morning."

"But there are only four meetings that are documented in the records that you have, June 9th, August 3rd, 14th and 28th. There would appear to be missing notes from two meetings."

"I would hesitate to say that there are notes missing. I would be more apt to say that when I was initially asked how many meetings occurred, I perhaps counted two other assessments that weren't mine."

"So, you may have been mistaken when you spoke to the police."

"I may have been."

"Okay. And when you met with the police on August 31st, you told them that August 14th was the first time that Jane disclosed to you that she was thinking about killing people. Do you remember hearing that on the audio tape this morning?"

"No. I can't remember what is on the tape."

"I'm going to suggest to you that Jane told you when you met her for the very first time on June 9th that she might take a knife to school and kill people who were bullying her and then kill herself."

"When I saw her on June 9th she stated that she was planning on using a kitchen knife to slit her throat and that she had plans to take a knife to school and kill bullies."

"Beth is one of the bullies at school. Right?"

"I don't know."

"Well, you saw the MSN texts that Jane brought to show you about the bullying, right?"

"I have those, yes."

"And is it your evidence that Jane did not make you aware that Beth was the person who was victimizing her at school and on the internet?"

"Actually, no. I understood that Jane and Beth were friends and that Jane was upset because Beth was no longer her friend."

"And you did not understand that Jane was upset because Beth had got a whole bunch of people at school to turn against her and dislike her. You were not aware of that?"

"No, I don't think I was aware of that."

"And it's your evidence that you did not believe that Beth was the person who was behind the internet bullying and the bullying that was going on at school?"

"That's not what I understood. No."

"When you say that's not what you understood, are you saying that Jane did not tell you those things?"

"No, she didn't tell me that Beth was directly responsible for the bullying. In fact, she named another person."

"Nadia Reeves. Right?"

"Yes."

"You know who Nadia Reeves is."

"Are you asking me that? Can I ask for some clarity around whether or not I'm permitted to discuss – and I'm not sure who I should be asking."

Justice Christie answered, "I take it that there may be another professional relationship here. Is that what I'm reading between the lines?"

"Yes," answered Tracey.

"All right," said His Honour. "I think at this stage you can proceed."

"You spoke with Jane of a person named Nadia Reeves," continued Mike.

"Yes, Jane brought the name to my attention."

"And in fact, after you went to the police and reported the thoughts that Jane shared with you, you were the subject of a complaint by Jane and her mother with respect to your having had some discussion with them about Nadia Reeves?"

"Yes, I believe that was the complaint," answered Tracy with a slight tremor in her voice.

"And to be specific, it was reported that you disclosed information about Nadia Reeves to Jane and perhaps to her mother as well."

Mike turned from the witness and with a flourish, said, "At this point in time, I'm going to ask her mother to leave the courtroom and wait outside, please."

As Helen left the courtroom, she gave Emily and Jack a small satisfied smile. When the door closed behind her, Mike continued.

"I'm going to suggest to you that you disclosed to Jane and her mother that you knew Nadia Reeves. True or false?"

"I was asked if I knew Nadia. I told them that I couldn't discuss other people.

I told them that I know lots of kids in lots of different capacities. I said that I'm in and out of schools all the time and that I have occasion to meet with kids in all kinds of different capacities. I also suggested that I couldn't discuss other people because I would get in trouble for that, and I suggested that you wouldn't want me talking about your issues with other people. That's what I said, which is standard. Kids often will ask us do you know so-and-so, or are you so-and-so's worker and we will often suggest that we can't discuss that."

"So, it's your evidence that you did not discuss any of Nadia Reeve's personal matters with Jane or her mother?"

"Well I did in the capacity that I said I can't talk about that with you because I know lots of kids. I said I've worked for CAS, the School Board, Support Services. I run into kids in all different capacities at all different times and I would know kids from different environments."

"So you did not tell Jane and her mother that Nadia had a history of bullying other kids?"

"No, I did not."

"You did not tell them that Nadia Reeves was involved with the Children's Aid Society and that her CAS worker is someone named Rita?"

"No I did not."

"You did not tell them that Nadia was involved in counseling with Kinark Child and Family Services?"

"No, I did not."

"And did you become aware that Jane does not even know Nadia? Was that conveyed to you?"

No."

"Did you read the MSN conversations?"

"I expressed at the time Jane gave these to me that I don't utilize MSN. I'm not familiar with it. I don't know how to decipher this. I don't know who's saying what. It is not in the realm of my understanding?

"Did you know that Nadia Reeves was one of the people who was bullying Jane on MSN within the texts that she disclosed to you?"

"I believe that's what Jane said to me, yes."

"Did she tell you that Beth Henderson put her up to it?"

"No."

"And did she tell you that, in fact, she did not even know Nadia Reeves and that this was just somebody who Beth had put up to bullying her?"

"No."

"Okay. So at the very first meeting that you have on June 9th, Jane shares some thoughts that she has about killing the bullies, right?"

"Yes."

"And before you met with her, did you review the intake forms, the Crisis Team Assessment Form prepared by Irene Vale when Jane first presented at the hospital?

"Briefly. That's part of what we're to do."

"So on the first page of that form there is a reference beside *Situational* that indicates *"bullying at school and on MSN."* So certainly by reviewing that report, you would be aware that the bullying at school and on MSN is an issue, right?"

"Yes."

"On the second page of the report under *Precipitating Events/ Current Stressors*, there is a note indicating *"patient states that a girl at school was spreading rumours."* Do you see that?"

"Yes, I see it."

"Okay, and on the third page of the *Crisis Team Assessment* under the category *Sexual and Physical Abuse*, it indicates *"Bullied at school and people on MSN."* Correct?"

"Yes, it says that."

"Now as a result of your meeting with Jane on June 9th, it is my understanding that you consulted with a psychiatrist. Was it Dr. Feldman?"

"No, it was Dr. Keita."

"So, I gather from looking at your notes, that Jane was placed on a Form 1 and accommodation within the inpatient setting was located for her at that time?"

"My knowledge is that after being placed on a Form 1, she was escorted to our Emergency Department and my involvement ceased."

"Was it not of interest to you to know how long she was kept for inpatient treatment pursuant to that Form 1?"

"She wasn't in my care at that point. Her care transferred from outpatient to inpatient."

"She came back under your care, right?"

"Yes. The next appointment that I had with her was August 3rd."

"So you did not see her from June 9th until August 3rd?"

"As best as I can remember and as is reflected in the chart, that would be correct."

"You told Detective Rutledge, when you were interviewed by him on August 31st, that you saw Jane on a weekly or bi-weekly basis. That clearly was not accurate, was it?"

"Well, our patient program is an outpatient, voluntary program. So, when a patient is transferred to another hospital for care, it's up to the patient to follow up with us."

"So you did not in fact see her on a weekly or bi-weekly basis, did you?"

"Well, no. I didn't see Jane on a bi-weekly or weekly basis because she was in an inpatient program."

"You told Detective Rutledge that upon release, she returned to your office on an outpatient basis. Correct?"

"At some point after her release, because I don't know how long she spent as an inpatient."

"I take it that you had no interest in finding out how long she was kept as an inpatient."

"We wouldn't normally pursue that information. We would wait for the child to return to us."

"Now she is back with you. You are seeing her again. Is it of no interest to know how long she was held on that Form 1?"

"Initially, my interest would be to check in with the patient to see what's going on, because there's been a big chunk of time that's passed."

"Do you think that the time she spent as an inpatient and the treatment she may or may not have received during that time might be useful information to you?"

"Yes."

"You did not have it."

"No."

"If I were to suggest to you that she spent a weekend, two days, at Toronto Hospital and was then released, is this the first time you are hearing this?"

"Yes."

"Now, at the conclusion of the August 14th meeting with Jane, she disclosed to you that she had been thinking about killing her boyfriend and Beth Henderson and you consulted with Dr. Feldman. Right?"

"Yes, as per our protocol."

"And you expressed to him the concerns that you had about the thoughts she had of killing people."

"Yes."

"Was Dr. Feldman the psychiatrist who was assigned to Jane's case?"

"Was he consulting? Is that what you mean?"

"Well, is there a particular psychiatrist who is responsible for each one of the patients?"

"It depends on how the patients come into our care. In this particular case, Dr. Feldman was involved with Jane. I asked him to see her on an outpatient basis for consultation. Dr. Keita was also involved, and Dr. Simpson on a consulted basis was involved as well."

Who is Dr. Simpson, wondered Jane, and how could someone I never met be involved with my care?

"Do you know which doctor was responsible for Jane's care?"

"I think that each doctor had some level of responsibility for her care."

"As far as you are aware, is it not the policy of the hospital to have one doctor assigned to each patient?"

"In Jane's case there were three psychiatrists involved. Dr. Keita issued the Form 1, Dr. Feldman was asked by me to do an outpatient assessment and Dr. Simpson was involved with consulting with me about my subsequent concerns."

Oh, thought Jane, Dr. Simpson talked to Tracey but not to me.

"So, on August 14th, after you met with Jane, you spoke with Dr. Feldman?"

"Yes I did."

"And Dr. Feldman told you that he did not feel Jane was capable of following through with the plan, right?"

"Yes, he did."

"And I understand that you expressed concern, to Dr. Feldman, that Jane's mother would not be able to call Youthdale."

"That's right. I did."

"Dr. Feldman did not feel that an admission was necessary, right?"

"I would suggest that you would have to ask him what his thoughts were."

"He did not admit Jane to hospital on August 14th, right?"

"That's right. He did not."

"Did you suggest to Dr. Feldman that he should admit her to hospital?"

"I suggested that I was very concerned and was seeking consultation."

"And that was your view as well at the conclusion of the meeting on June 9th. Correct?"

"Yes."

"At the conclusion of the August 28th meeting, did you again consult with Dr. Feldman?"

"Yes."

"And with Jane's mother as well?"

"Yes."

"Do you recall a discussion taking place between yourself, Jane and her mother, when they were considering moving Jane away from the school that Beth Henderson and the other bullies attended and enrolling her in another school? Do you remember that?"

"I do know that we discussed that. I don't know for certain that it was on the 28th."

"I am going to suggest to you that in response to their suggestion, you told Helen and Jane that moving to a different school would be a mistake and that it would be better for her to stay at the same school as the bullies."

"I do recall that discussion and I have never denied it. My response was that I think it's least intrusive and better to try and work out the issues with the school and if you can't do that then try and move to another school. That's what I said. The issue was raised and my recommendation was to try and work it out with the school personnel. And usually, best practice is we will say to people if you need our support at one of those school meetings we'll try and accommodate that."

"Okay, and when you spoke to Helen Collins on August 28th, she told you that she was aware of her daughter's thoughts about Beth and that she had discouraged her from following through with her plan because then Beth would be seen as the victim when all along, she has been the bully. You made a note of that conversation."

"Yes."

"So certainly, on August 28th, you were aware that Beth was one of the bullies."

"Yes."

"In your consultation with Dr. Feldman on August 28th, did you again speak to him about inpatient treatment?"

"I gave him an update and stated my concerns and sought support around what should happen or how we can be supportive."

"Dr. Feldman was not going to admit Jane on a Form 1 to be treated as an inpatient at that time?"

"No but he continued to support a Youthdale crisis admission."

"But he was not prepared to admit her."

"I would suggest that you would have to ask him that."

"Well, you were there speaking with him about this at that point in time, right?"

"Yes, and what he said was, direct Mrs. Collins to call Youthdale."

Emily hoped that Mike would ask Ms. Hogan why she did not phone Helen if Dr. Feldman had instructed her to do so. She knew that her sister always complied with instructions given by doctors and counsellors. If told to call Youthdale, she certainly would have done so.

Why call the police, wondered Jack.

"You knew that Dr. Feldman was not going to admit Jane to hospital, so when did you first go to the police?"

"On the 29th I met with my team for clinical supervision and presented my concerns. The team included Dr. Simpson, a psychiatrist who is the Clinical Director of the program. The case was discussed and the team decided that I was to contact the police."

Why was Helen not on the team, wondered Emily and Jack.

"You were concerned that Jane's mother was not going to take her and admit her voluntarily to the Youthdale Crisis Centre. Correct?"

"I was concerned about that."

"And had Jane been admitted to Youthdale, at that point in time, those concerns would have been certainly not as urgent as you felt they were. Correct?"

"I think it would have provided a level of safety because Jane would have been in an inpatient environment. So I think that the element of Jane being in the community and being a risk to herself and others would have been eliminated."

It would have been eliminated if she had changed schools, thought Emily and Jack. Why did she not suggest this simple solution, they wondered.

"Did you address the possibility of Dr. Simpson signing a Form 1 and having Jane admitted as an inpatient? Did you raise that with Dr. Simpson?"

"I was given direction by my Clinical Director."

"According to your notes, Dr. Simpson advised you to call the police and report Jane's homicidal plan to them. Correct?"

"The team decided. I was given the direction from Dr. Simpson after the team consultation. So there were actually five heads kind of involved in that decision at one level or another, but the ultimate direction came from Dr. Simpson."

I would like to knock those five heads together, thought Emily who could barely control her anger.

"So, you phoned the police on August 29th and met with Detectives Rutledge and Williams on the 31st."

"Yes, we met in my office with my manager present."

"In the audio taped interview with the police, you told them about the extensive amount of bullying that Jane had suffered during the past school year. Do you remember telling them about that?"

"I remember suggesting that there had been a history of bullying."

"You told the police that Beth was a friend who had betrayed her and was responsible for getting other kids to dislike her, or words to that effect. Do you remember saying that?"

"I don't recall saying that specifically."

"Okay. You do not know Beth Henderson and never told Jane that you knew her, did you?"

"No."

"You never said anything to Jane that would suggest to her that you were going to tell Beth Henderson about the thoughts that Jane shared with you, did you?"

"When we initially have contact with our clients we talk about confidentiality and in what context confidentiality can be breached. That's standard practice. We do it at the beginning of every session without fail. It's just rote at this point.

No, you do not, thought Jane.

"So with regard to that, I would have suggested that there are instances when confidentiality may be breached. If you're going to hurt yourself or someone else, if you're going on a self-destructive path and you're going to leave my office and do something. And usually, with children, I will give an example. I'll say something like, if you're going to rob a bank or if you're going to do something that would be harmful or contrary to the law, then we do have a duty to report. I would have suggested that sometimes we are to warn the intended victim. Sometimes we have to call the police, sometimes we tell parent and sometimes we call Children's Aid. It just depends on how we're directed and what makes best sense. So, in that context, that would have been addressed."

Liar, thought Jane in surprise. You never said anything like that to me! She was shocked to hear an adult lie with such impunity on the witness stand.

"Specifically," continued Mike, "I'm going to tell Beth Henderson about your plan?"

"No. That was never said."

"You are basically a crisis worker whose job is to help the children and adolescents who are coming to see you, and I take it that you want them to be open with you and tell you about the thoughts they are having. You want to know about drug use, the relationships they have with family, friends and people that they come into contact with throughout the course of their lives. And patients holding things in, who don't openly share the issues that they are confronting in their lives cannot be helped, right?"

"We can only work with information that we get."

"Do you tell children and adolescents that you want them to be open with you?"

"We encourage kids to feel as though it's a safe place to talk, yes."

But it's not a safe place to talk, thought Jane.

A safe place to talk, thought Emily in disgust. Are you frikking kidding me!

"As far as you are aware, Jane does not have any sort of – up until she was arrested by police – she does not have any sort of animosity toward you that you are aware of?" asked Mike.

"Not that I was aware of. No."

"Are you familiar with a movie called *The Nightmare Before Christmas*? Have you seen it?"

"No."

"It is an animated movie produced and directed by Tim Burton. Does it ring any bells?"

"I've not seen the movie. I think I've seen kid's shirts and such with characters from that movie but I'm not familiar with it."

"Would it surprise you to know that Jane's plan bears a striking similarity to the plot lines of this movie?"

"I'm not sure I understand what you mean. Would I have guessed that or did I know that? No, I wouldn't have known that."

"Are you familiar with another Tim Burton movie called *Corpse Bride*?"

"No."

"Did Jane tell you that she had an interest in horror movies?"

"No."

Glancing at his watch, Mike turned to Justice Christie. "I wonder if we could end there and perhaps address the issue of my client's bail?"

His Honour replied, "Sure. Miss Collins, I am adjourning your trial on this charge to the 7th of June, 2007, 9:30 a.m. Ms. Hogan, you are still subject to the subpoena and must return on June 7th to continue your evidence at 9:30 in the morning. Court is adjourned."

Jane, Emily and Jack joined Helen who had been waiting nervously outside the courtroom to give evidence. Her disappointment at not being called as a witness was overshadowed by the disheartening news that the trial was to continue the following week. In the interim, Ms. Parson had agreed to relax some of the harsh bail conditions that Jane had endured for nine long months.

"Maybe I'll be able to go to the Dairy Queen in Toxteth," Jane said hopefully.

"Will the police get a copy of the revised bail conditions?" asked Ms. Parson breezily. "That's how we do it in Bantry." Then she and Mike Rivers met privately behind closed doors.

When Mike emerged, he explained to Helen and Jane that the Crown had offered to withdraw the charge if they would simply provide a letter signed by their family doctor, stating that Jane was being seen on a regular basis for counselling.

"This would be a guaranteed result," said Mike. "You should accept the offer."

"We shouldn't have to provide them with anything," argued Helen. "They probably realize that they don't have a case and that Jane should never have been charged in the first place. They're just trying to save face. Jane and I want a chance to take the witness stand and give evidence. The judge needs to hear the truth and Tracey Hogan should be charged with perjury."

In early June, Mike was able to persuade Helen and Jane to accept the Crown's offer. He understood their reluctance but believed that it was an easy resolution that would spare them another miserable, stressful day in court.

When Helen arrived home from work on Monday, the fifth of June, she was met at the door by Jane.

"Mr. Rivers called," she said. "He needs me to sign a consent form so Dr. March can fax him the letter we need for court. He wants us to meet him in Newton."

"Oh no," sighed Helen, "I'm so tired and I've just come from Newton." She phoned Mike and agreed to meet at the Tim Hortons doughnut shop on First Street that evening.

"Can I get some Timbits and a drink while we're there?" asked Jane.

When Helen and Jane climbed out of the car in front of Tim Hortons, they were greeted by a biker, dressed in black leather, leaning on a Harley Davidson. It was Mike. Jane felt very important as she signed the consent form on the seat of his motorcycle. With that, Mike fastened his helmet and roared off down First Street.

The following afternoon, as Emily sat reading the newspaper and sipping tea, she was interrupted by a frantic phone call from Mike's office. They had not received the letter from Jane's doctor and Helen could not be reached. Emily phoned Dr. March's office and was told that it would be necessary for

Jane to be seen by the doctor before the letter would be written. She then phoned the Newton courthouse and had her sister paged. Helen, who had been recording evidence in a trial, left the courtroom and raced to get Jane from school, then rushed her over to Dr. March's office. The letter was faxed just in time to be given to the Crown the following day. Everyone breathed a sigh of relief.

On June 7th, Helen, Jane, Jack and Emily met at the courthouse believing that Jane's charge was about to be withdrawn by the Crown. Mike met with Ms. Parson and handed her the letter from Jane's doctor, as requested on May 31st.

"Here comes Mr. Rivers," said Jane. "Wow, his face is so red! He looks really mad!"

"The Crown has backed out of the deal and refuses to withdraw the charge," he announced.

"But they promised that if we brought them the letter, I could go home and this would be over," said Jane, disappointed and confused.

"Please sir," said Dorothy to the Wizard. "I've done as you asked. Here is the broomstick of the Wicked Witch. So I would like you to keep your promise to me, if you please sir."

"Not so fast," bellowed the Wizard. "I will have to give the matter a little more thought. Go away and come back tomorrow."

"Tomorrow! Oh please, I want to go home now."

"I can't believe it," Mike was saying. "Now, Parson is offering to "stay" the charge."

"What does that mean?" asked Jack.

Helen answered, "I think it means that they wouldn't pursue the charge at this time but they could decide to bring it forward at any point in the future. It would remain unresolved and hanging over Jane's head. Is that right Mike?"

"Yeah," he sighed. "I don't like it."

"Why won't they withdraw the charge?" asked Helen. "I don't understand why they changed their minds."

"The explanation given to me by Ms. Parson was, and I quote, "the Crown will only accept certain outcomes in order to avoid civil exposure," Mike told them. "And I would testify under oath that those were her exact words to me."

"You mean they won't withdraw the charge because they're afraid of being sued?" asked Emily.

"Yep, that's right," said Mike. "I don't think we should accept their offer to stay the charge. I have another idea. I'm going to propose a "non-suit" to the judge."

Mike explained that he would be suggesting to the judge that since the Crown could not provide sufficient evidence, the case should be withdrawn.

Justice Christie gave the matter some consideration, but in the end, decided that there was sufficient evidence to proceed with the trial.

"Maybe that's a good thing," said Jane, during a break outside the courtroom. "I want to explain what really happened. It's only fair that my mom and I get to tell the judge our side of the story."

"This has nothing to do with fairness, Jane," explained Mike. "It's very easy to say the wrong thing when you are on the witness stand. The Crown will ask questions designed to trick you into saying the wrong thing."

"But I'll just tell the truth," said Jane.

"Okay," said Mike. "Pretend that you are on the witness stand and I am Ms. Parson. Miss Collins, why did you say you were going to kill Beth Henderson?"

"I didn't mean it," responded Jane without hesitation. "It was just a fantasy."

"No, no, no," said Mike. "Wrong, wrong, wrong! You should never admit saying that. Do you see how easy it would be to say the wrong thing?"

Jane began to cry. "I'm afraid to take the witness stand but I need to tell the judge my side of the story. I don't know what to do." A small tear rolled down her cheek.

"Take it easy Jane," Mike said. "The judge gave me a nod a few minutes ago and, if I am reading him correctly, I don't think you need to give evidence. I could be wrong but I think the judge understands and it would be a mistake for you to say anything. But it's your decision. You are my client and I take direction from you. I could be wrong about the judge."

"That's not fair," said Emily. "Jane is young and inexperienced. What do you suggest?"

"I am not going to make the decision," said Mike.

"I don't want to say anything, I'm scared that I might make a mistake," said Jane. "So, no, I won't do it."

When court resumed, Mike advised that he would be calling no witnesses and Justice Christie retired to his chambers to compose his decision.

30.

Tell Me When It's Over

After an excruciating wait, His Honour Justice Christie re-entered the courtroom. The anticipation was palpable as Jane and her family hoped he was about to put them out of their misery. Please, oh please, say not guilty, Jane thought desperately. Justice Christie carefully unfolded his glasses, placed them on the end of his nose and began reading aloud:

"I am prepared to deal with the matter. The young person and her parent are both present. This decision then follows the completion of the defendant young person's trial on one charge of threatening, contrary to s. 264.1(1)(a). The Crown's case rests solely on the evidence of the Child and Youth Worker, Tracey Hogan. The defence has elected to call no evidence..."

Jack, as the owner of a market research company, tested public reaction to products and television advertisements then presented his findings to clients. Mindful of the fact that they were nervous and anxious to hear the bottom line, he always provided the final results first and then afterward gave details of how they had been determined. This judge was not so considerate. As Jack listened to him ramble on interminably, he wondered bitterly why this civil servant was inflicting so much agony on a fourteen-year-old girl and her mother. It was cruel and unnecessary.

Justice Christie spoke of "reasonable doubt" and "balance of probabilities." He cited precedent-setting court cases. On and on he droned, reiterating Tracey Hogan's testimony. Phrases such as "self-inflicted knife wound," "thoughts of killing her boyfriend and an ex-girlfriend," "suicidal and paranoid thoughts," "broke into a motor vehicle and started setting fires," "gave explicit and graphic indications of how she might torture and kill Beth H.," felt like vicious stab wounds to Helen's heart. She could barely endure such a barrage. The floor appeared to move in sickening waves and her heartbeat was so rapid and violent that she feared a heart attack. The judge's words seemed to indicate that her daughter was guilty. She wanted desperately to wrap her arms around Jane and protect her from the torment.

The grandstanding continued. "Ms. Hogan presented her evidence in a clear fashion, accessing her notes and points in detail," declared Justice Christie, pausing to peer over his glasses at his captive audience. "She expressed some lack of recollection on a few details, but aside from noting that her primary training was in the criminology field, I was left with no other caution going to her truthfulness or the accuracy of her evidence."

Oh no, thought Emily in dismay, he believes Hogan was a credible witness! He must have slept through Mike's cross-examination!

His Honour then began mulling over the "actus reus" and "mens rea" of the offence.

Have mercy! Now he's torturing us with arcane Latin terms, thought Emily as she wiped the perspiration from her brow. Just get to the point!

As Jane listened to the judge, she was reminded of a sickening roller coaster ride she had once taken as a small child. "I want to get off Mommy!" she had screamed.

It seemed as though Justice Christie was deliberately pro-longing her suffering. Valiantly she tried not to cry when he made reference to Tracey's evidence as if it was entirely factual. She reproached herself for not having had the courage to stand up and tell him the truth. Her stomach churned menacingly and she imagined herself vomiting in the courtroom. How embar-rassing that would be! An unpleasant coppery taste in her dry mouth made her long for a sip of water from the paper cup on the desk but she resisted for fear that it might make her sick. Miser-able and uncomfortable, she was aware of the sweat-soaked shirt sticking to her back and the damp hair plastered to her forehead. She felt unable to fill her lungs with sufficient air and feared an impending panic attack or fainting spell.

"I am left in no doubt that the defendant intended the threats to be taken seriously," proclaimed the judge, "but only in the sense of getting help. I find support for this conclusion in the opinion of the second psychiatrist who, in the Crown's evidence, did not think that the defendant was capable of following through with the threats, a mere one day before the team meeting, at which he was apparently not present, which led to the conclusion to engage the police. I am left with a strong reasonable doubt..."

Finally, Justice Christie became silent. Mike Rivers clicked his pen and set a file folder in front of Jane. "YOU WIN," he wrote.

The cowardly Lion shook with fear. "Tell me when it's over," he said to Dorothy, Scarecrow and Tin Man. "I want to go home."

The monstrous head of the Wizard loomed above them. "And what have you to say for yourself lion?" he bellowed.

The terrified lion fainted and fell to the ground.

Dorothy gasped and looked up at the Wizard defiantly. "You should be ashamed of yourself!" she said. "Frightening him like that, when he came to you for help."

31.

Epilogue

It is now late summer 2013 and Helen's three sons have moved forward with their lives. James and his fiancée graduated from Algonquin College and share an apartment in Ottawa. Joe, an RCMP officer, makes his home in northern British Columbia with his wife Kate. Chris completed his program at Seneca College and has an Information Technology career in Toronto.

After graduating from University, Mark took a position with the Federal government, and Jason is a student at the Toronto Film School. They live in Toronto and recently celebrated their seventh anniversary together.

Emily and Jack march with PFLAG in the Toronto Gay Pride parade every year to promote equal rights for gay, lesbian, bisexual and transgender people.

Stephen has moved to a beautiful group home in Allerton but spends most weekends with his parents. He uses a keyboard with voice output and meets regularly with a group of autistic friends who also use supported typing to communicate. Their group is called *Bridges over Barriers*. Together they share coping strategies, ideas and audacious goals.

Outwardly, Helen's life has not changed. She continues to live in Allerton, work at the Newton Courthouse and spend evenings and weekends typing transcripts in her bedroom. Both she and her daughter have been diagnosed with Post-Traumatic Stress Disorder. She struggles to maintain her composure and hide her feelings of anger, bitterness and resentment when working with certain judges, lawyers and one particular JP. Watching hardened criminals afforded more compassion and much better treatment than Jane, at age fourteen, is exceedingly painful for her. She suffers from major health problems and no longer enjoys social gatherings or vacations but prefers to stay safely at home with her daughter.

Jane and her friend Daniel parted company in 2007 and shortly thereafter, he dropped out of school and vanished from her life. She completed grade twelve at Allerton High School in June 2011, a year after the bullies at St. Joan of Arc. Initially, she told her family that she would not be attending the graduation ceremony but changed her mind just hours in advance. Only Helen, Emily and Jack were available on such short notice.

The atmosphere inside Allerton High School was noisy and festive as Emily and Jack searched among throngs of happy graduates for Jane and Helen. Everywhere they looked, young, fresh-faced students were chatting excitedly among themselves, hugging, kissing, offering congratulations to one another and posing together for photographs. Jane stood apart from the others, looking radiant in the blue cap and gown, her long hair cascading down her back in luxuriant curls. Emily and Jack wondered why she was not the most popular girl in the school.

"You look so pretty," Emily commented as she snapped a photograph. "I'll take another one. This time don't hang your head. Throw your shoulders back and show some self-confidence."

The ceremony was long and tedious. Predictably, the principal, vice-principal and teachers hugged their favourite students and the crowd hooted and cheered for the popular graduates and those who had won awards. When Jane walked onto the stage to accept her diploma, she received no friendly hugs, just a perfunctory, half-hearted handshake. There was a polite smattering of applause as she rushed down the steps so quickly that Emily had no time to take a photograph. Each of the other students had posed proudly on stage, but not Jane.

After the class of 2011 had marched down the centre aisle to the tune of "Pomp and Circumstance," everyone gathered in the gym to chat and feast upon a lovely spread prepared by the culinary arts students, but Jane was eager to leave. As her uncle eyed the tempting hors d'oeuvres, Nanaimo bars and chocolate brownies, she took him by the arm and suggested, "Let's just go to Tim Hortons for coffee and doughnuts."

Throughout the entire evening, only one person, a former St. Joseph elementary school teacher, had stopped to say hello to Jane. During her five years of high school, she had made no friends.

Jane is different from the other graduates. She has no plans for the future and has not applied for admission to a college or university. She relies heavily upon her mother for companionship and cannot bear to be away from home, the little bungalow in Allerton, or her mother, for more than a few hours. She continues to require medication for panic attacks and extreme night terrors. Her world is small.

In 2007 Emily and Jack retained a high profile lawyer to represent Jane and Helen in a civil lawsuit. A Claim was filed against Southern Ontario Hospital, Tracey Hogan, Dr. Joanne Simpson and the Police Department. They believed the Crown to be equally culpable, guilty of malicious prosecution, but were advised that suing the Attorney General of Ontario would be prohibitively expensive and probably futile. The original purpose of the Claim was to obtain an apology in the form of funding for Jane's education. Six years and $200,000 later, the case remains unresolved. A trial date has been set for November, 2015, at which time; Jane will be twenty-three years old.

www.ingramcontent.com/pod-product-compliance
Lightning Source LLC
Chambersburg PA
CBHW051754040426
42446CB00007B/354